Amazing Real Hope
A Journey to Freedom from Religion and Addiction

Troy Ingenhuett

ISBN:9781791716233
ISBN-13:9781791716233

DEDICATION

The book you are now going to enjoy I dedicate to the two most amazing influences my life knows: my daughter, Tyler and my son, Thomas. For you this book marks my infrangible love. I cannot change Daddy's past, but I can write it to create your future. You two are my inspiration of **Amazing Real Hope**. *I love you so much!!*

Daddy

"Most will think this is just another book - it's not, it's a story of a life of serious addiction. Only a mother, whose child has been through a similar situation, will believe my pain, endless blaming myself, hours praying and crying out to God, and numerous hidden fears all covered up with a smile.

My son's memory of details, the way he has painted this picture, and the drawing power of his words are just amazing. You will want to buy several copies to give to others who might have a loved one caught up in an addiction - it will give them **Amazing Real Hope**!"

~ Diane Abel - Mama

"If you've ever questioned the truth about what you've been taught or struggled with the God of your understanding this book should be your next read. Troy Ingenhuett does a phenomenal job eloquently expressing his truth and his heart that will absolutely keep you turning the pages. **Amazing Real Hope** is truly captivating."

~ Megan Britt

"**Amazing Real Hope** offers hurting people a glimpse into the mind of one who has experienced hurt, pain and confusion and his description is not just that of a onetime experience; he draws a picture with his words of what he's experienced from childhood to right now. Troy lays himself bare in the hope of touching lives, not with just another formula but with **Amazing Real Hope**!"

~ Pat Wright - Bible Teacher

"Encouraging, uplifting, life changing…Break your chains of condemnation from sin and addiction by understanding your Father's Grace. Travel with Troy through struggles and realization in his story of **Amazing Real Hope**."

~ Carol Davis - I was there

"An excellent read you just can't put down. A modern genius and nothing less than exceptional"

~ Jerry Fox

"Smile, laugh, cry and Thank God in this intriguing, exciting journey. You will fall in love with Troy, experience sympathy, empathy and end up in God's pure love. It's a can't put down must read book."

~ Alisha Yeager

"*This writer kept my interest from beginning to end. A set sail in alignment with your God-given Destiny guides us to truth and righteousness through this book of* **Amazing Real Hope**. *What a powerful story of a mother's love that will challenge mothers to never give up. This is a true story of* **Amazing Real Hope***!*"

~ *Jeannie Ross - Family friends of more than 40 years*

"*Thank you Troy for baring your heart and soul in this writing. Your sincere delivery of the experiences is intriguing.* **Amazing Real Hope** *is destined to bring hope and significance to countless men.*"

~ *Clyde E. Drake*

FOREWORD

My wife, Johnna and I were employed at Canaan Land Bible Training Center by Brother Mac and Ms. Sandra Gober when we met Troy. We wore many hats while developing the greatest relationships with so many people. Some of those relationships have made monumental marks in our lives such as it is with Troy.

The events and our introduction were just as he has described in this book along with many unmentioned great moments. His friendship helped chart our personal journey to Freedom and Grace. It is an honor to write the forward for this extraordinary book of **Amazing Real Hope**.

I have known Troy for years and years and he has a charismatic way of explaining things, this book is nothing short of who he is. Troy is always energetic and enlightening in his conversations. You will find this book the same, full of energy and very enlightening. He has a way of talking you through situations so that you can see the beauty in what's going on and captures you to exciting expectation for what's to come. As a matter fact Troy would talk to me about Grace and the finished work of the Cross over and over and over again. I just didn't see it, but I recall how I would jump with excitement on the inside every time we talked. Then, as Troy always insisted, I went to the Bible to find out for myself. I too ended up getting radically set free and saw Grace from cover to cover. Our life has never been the same!

I believe as you read this book you too will experience this walk- through Christianity and religion and into Freedom. You will see the trap set up by performance-based Christianity and move into the freedom of the finished work of the Cross. Inevitably you will see that no matter where you've been or where you go God is with you and His hand is always on you.

Troy's journey proves in an amazing way that you cannot escape God's Amazing Grace! You are never too far for His **Amazing Real Hope** *to flourish and grow in your life like never imagined. It starts right here in this journey by opening your heart and mind to the possibility that you don't know everything, just like I did.*

I encourage you to sit back with a cup of coffee or tea and enjoy the journey of **Amazing Real Hope**! *Love to you all! His Grace is more than sufficient for us all. You are safe!*

Phil Bevilacqua
aka Pops

Grace and Peace to You All
Phil and Johnna Bevilacqua
334-365-8672

Grace Life Church   www.churchgonewild.tv
This is Us Life Coaching   www.thisisuscoaching.com

INTRODUCTION

This book contains intimate knowledge of my life I have not shared with anyone. Divine purpose lies within you. My hope is that purpose is revealed as you enjoy reading, and that you gain freedom in my discoveries. You will see things that influenced my devalued perspective, my poor self-image and how I struggled to find acceptance. My desire is that questions regarding God's acceptance are answered.

It is not necessary to strive for God's acceptance. We need not toil about being in His will. We ARE THE WILL of GOD. Everything He has done is just for us. We are His will, His purpose and His pleasure. There is nothing God wants us to do FOR Him. However, there is an amazing destiny He desires to enjoy WITH us.

*It is not the shifting of the wind that determines our destiny; it is the setting of our sail. And that destiny is filled with **AMAZING REAL HOPE** !*

Troy Ingenhuett

CHAPTER 1

I remember details of the week after Valentine's Day of 1997. A few hours before I was expected to be at the office, the life I had created crumbled out of control. I became emptied of every ounce of humanity. I was out of the tub without my towel and lying on the living room floor. It was an elegant and beautiful 1,100 square foot luxury one-bedroom apartment near the Dallas Cowboy's practice field. Just two weeks prior she was with me and we planned her soon arrival. She was who had become my identity and certainly the wife who would never fail or reject me. After all she had more than proven it over the thirteen years of chaos, instability and emotional turmoil. This is the inevitable when trusting in a drug addict.

There was no furniture and no décor. The apartment was empty just like me. Everything would be moved in along with my gorgeous wife in two weeks. Meanwhile I slept on the floor in front of an old turn knob tube television with tin foil wrapped around the antenna. I remember her smile seeing where we would move and attempt to create a home all over again. I wept uncontrollably and wailed words as if I practiced them often, yet it had been almost fifteen years since I prayed or acknowledged God. *"God, please help me! What have I done?"*

The night before I joined a co-worker at his bachelor apartment for drinks, dinner and multiple games of pool. I drank more than I should when expecting to drive, and certainly much more after not sleeping for seven days. I tried to forget the words, *"I want a divorce"*, and did what became my natural response to undesirable emotions. I smoked crack and I smoked more. Just as an aspirin cures a headache, I discovered, about 15 years prior, how to medicate feelings. But now, for what seemed a terminal heartache, it wasn't working. My self- reliance in which I believed to be strong and undefeatable was the essence by which I sculpted the delusion of failed satisfaction. Until this devastation I considered my life acceptable. My solution was simple. Drugs dulled my senses and I didn't have to face life. Early on it seemed to work. However, my self-reliance, determination, talent and even personal convictions were no competition against the gorilla grip the drugs had on me. Although I didn't see it myself, others pinned addiction long before I personally faced defeat.

My co-worker almost begged for me to stay and offered accommodations perhaps more comfortable than my own. However, my stubbornness was aroused and insisted I drive back to my lonely apartment. Feeling invincible, I took off. Only a mile or so from my destination, I instantly fell asleep at the wheel. Vaguely I recall the short distance to the curve in the road, only because I later learned from the officer who investigated the vacated accident that my '91 Chevrolet Cavalier went over the curb, down an embankment and up the other side. I called the sheriff's department and told them a friend borrowed the car and I needed to retrieve my personal belongings.

"It appears as if the driver didn't see the curve in the road and continued straight. The car became airborne and landed on top of a concrete wall that retained a 24-inch culvert. The engine and transmission were pushed through the hood. The driver broke the steering wheel with his chest. A witness says he ran across the five- lane highway into the river. We looked for hours and even ran the dogs but found nobody. We were certain he died and was carried down river."

The water was cold. It was near the last week of February 1997, and there had not been any warm weather. The Trinity River wasn't swift as I recall. My left shoulder hurt tremendously. I could only assume it hit the steering wheel during the impact. I do remember reaching the street to meet a man who stopped because of witnessing my accident. I assessed no other car was involved. Frantically I asked the man to give me a ride to the gas station just up the road.

"I better call for help", he exclaimed as he dialed his cell phone. Because I was drunk my first instinct was to dart across the road and forge through the grass. I set out to cross what I perceived to be a drainage ditch. On the other side, I made my way up stream. My next memory was waking high above the ground on a railroad trestle.

Under me was what appeared to be a gravel pit. I surveyed my surroundings and saw flashing red-blue and amber lights in the distance, and what appeared to be a small white match box car being pulled up a flatbed wrecker. There were flashlights all over the bank of the river searching for a lifeless body floating down stream. That not so lifeless body was me. This was not the first time God chose to save my life and would prove not to be the last.

Frantic and delirious, I searched for civilization. It was not yet sunrise and a passerby stopped to give me a ride to my apartment. I headed to the bathroom and caught a glimpse of the digital clock that sat on the bedroom floor next to a pair of lonely shoes. The time was 4:27 a.m. *"I made it",* I said to myself as I dropped to the floor, lifted my head and pushed myself to my knees. I don't recall crying for many years. I am fairly certain not one tear had traveled my cheeks in more than fifteen years. I was twenty-nine and would be prosperous if it hadn't been for addiction gripping my soul.

The tears I felt were not of sorrow or from pain. As I recall this early morning could only be described as peaceful, maybe glorious. The effect of incalculable amounts of cocaine, marijuana, alcohol and whatever else I consumed the past seven days was gone.

Instantaneously I was sober. I remember this moment as if it just occurred. Completely sober, detoxed and fresh it was as if I had never made the decision that wrecked my life and broke the hearts of many whom attempted to love me. I was a tragic disappointment to life.

CHAPTER 2

My decision to curse God and get high changed a world for generations to come. Choices are what forms the world we live in and sets the mold for our future. Where would we be if Jesus had made just one decision that opposed His purpose? Today I write hoping to improve our lives, our families and this world. The fact is we are all world changers.

June 2, 1997, our divorce was final. Twenty years later and words I spoke to my precious wife just seven days prior to the accident still haunt me. I may never heal from the horror I put myself through. My arrogance, pride and stupidity formed from anger, resentment and blame created it all. I was haunted with anger prior to my 15th birthday. Although I do not intend to write my life story in detail, it will be of necessity to cover a few things to give you an understanding of why and how I made many decisions along life's journey. I will also unveil how concepts in mainstream Christianity have injured the hearts and lives of many people like me. You may have seen this effect in the lives of people you know. Traditions and philosophies affect us and sculpt our lives and our world. Not all these are negative and certainly they have not affected everyone in the same tragic manner I experienced. My life is the direct result of my own decisions. I believe my decisions are the result of my perceptions. I believe many perceptions are results of our environments. Let me explain using the life of a Prince.

A beautiful young lady is giving birth to her first child. However, not one person is with her. She is alone. The young lady was abandoned at the ER entrance and she is beyond her senses. Her long brown hair is matted and appears to not have been washed in weeks. Her sweet olive complexion is hidden by grime and oil from not bathing. Her beautiful brown eyes, that stole her Daddy's heart, are glazed and lost. Needle tracks and sores are evident on her arms and legs from the massive amount of heroine she has used over the last year. She disappeared a week before her eighteenth birthday.

The child's complexion is much darker than hers and his hair is kinky. He is the son of a black man. Just down the hall is an elegant well- dressed dynasty with child number three about to join The Royal Family. The father is here for a government meeting. Because a child will soon join them, the family servants and education team came with King Mustofa and Queen Mahafanot. The King and Queen of Urburnoto, Africa gave birth to their beautiful new baby boy at 2:47 a.m. in Washington, D.C. The entire family is celebrating as the delivery doctor congratulates the children and staff waiting in the family room. A new Prince has joined the world and King Mustofa is shouting with great joy!

Suddenly a very alarming cry came over the intercom and the celebration silenced immediately. "Dr. G, Dr. G! Room 101" Dr. Garcia spun and launched to a sprint toward the ER. He knew instantly things were not good by the quiver in Nurse

Jackson's voice echoing the halls as she screamed through the intercom.

The caring King curiously followed the doctor to see if there is anything he can do to assist. King Mustofa isn't a stranger to tragedy or death. When he was a child his country was in war with neighboring rebels. The rebels were no match for the army his great grandfather built by bringing in special force retirees from the United States to assist in training. The King's father continued to increase the effectiveness of the military. However, the rebels caused great atrocities to their neighboring countrymen. His father took him to assist with medical supplies and personnel. The King gave consideration to his seeing death and blood shed to encourage the Prince to preserve and protect his family, palace and country. This experience left an indelible mark on the Prince. He became an even greater loving King than his father ever hoped! The sight of the beautiful lonely and now lifeless girl caused a tsunami of these memories.

Dr. Garcia rapidly clamped and snipped the umbilical cord. There were no nurse's hands available. They were performing every effort to resuscitate the young "Jane Doe." Dr. G placed the just born baby boy in the hands of the King. The King looked down his heart almost skipped a beat. A single tear ran down both cheeks as he whispered. "A Prince is born. This is my son." He held the baby close to his heart and cleaned him with his tears. The tears he wept dripped on the infant's tiny head. "You are the son of a King! My son, no matter what the price I will pay more than double! You are perfect, without blame and you are mine. You are a Prince!"

Although the King whispered, his passion echoed in the heavens. This is Loving – Kindness, the heart of God.

King Mustofa soon appeared in the waiting room with two baby boys nestled in his arms. He announced to his children and staff. "Today God has given us twins!"

The authorities granted the King the adoption of the baby boy. He paid more than double and made a large contribution to the hospital. He built an entire new facility specializing in the treatment and recovery of drug addicted mothers. The boys grew up as brothers. No one in the world knew anything but the King's declaration. The baby boy born of the young heroin addict only knew the life of a Prince. He is the son of a King. The King's authority, all his riches and all he is belongs to his children. Equal to his brother in every way he would only know one thing, "I'm the son of The King! I have all that he has, and I will live to be all that he is. He is my Daddy and I am his son." This is his identity!

No one or anything can change the redemption of the King. This is what God did through Christ. He paid more than double! You are a Child of The King! You are redeemed! The tears of God have declared of you, "This is my child!" There is nothing anyone or anything can do to change the declaration of THE KING!

If anyone placed doubt in the Princes' mind, his philosophies may have been affected. Given his authority, his skewed philosophies would affect the Palace, the Kingdom, his country and the world. What if those closest to him taught him his rambunctious behavior offended his father and he would have to grovel for forgiveness or lose his birthright? What if he was told his father would disown him every time he misbehaves and if he didn't bow down and give praise then his Daddy would not grant him access to the gifts he had *received. Even worse, his Father would curse him and bless nothing he does. What if the young Prince believed the only time the King will have anything to do with him is when he is as his brother?*

Suppose he is told his brother is perfect, he'll never be perfect and he's nothing like him. The only way he can be with the King is to admit he is unworthy, and grovel for his mercy, and plead for his grace so he will see him. Sound familiar?

Unfortunately, these types of ideas, concepts and philosophies shape the world we live in today. We find that these anti-Christ teachings have corrupted the church since its establishment. These ideas destroy desire to be near God.

I have a personal reservation for the word "Christian." I was told Gandhi once said he would be a Christian himself if he could find but one. People have been killed, crushed and mostly shunned all in the name of "Christianity." The horrific truth is that many have perceived it was God. Those who proclaim being ostracized have been deceived to believe it is what God desired. I have heard many people say, "The greatest victory the devil ever had is to convince people he didn't exist." Well, I absolutely disagree. His greatest victory has been his ability to discount Jesus! My hope is that my writings create in you an unmovable, irrevocable, life changing encounter with the Love of God.

CHAPTER 3

Sunday evening, September 1982, around 6:00 p.m. there was the typical excitement in the air at **Church of Living Waters** Rosenberg, Texas. We anticipated Robert to move forward and begin to strum captivating chords as he encouraged the congregation to join him in worship. He always led the dynamic praise and worship team with enthusiasm. My favorite was to hear him dance across the strings of his Gibson electric guitar, playing some awesome solo envied by Rock and Roll's greatest. For several years, I imagined that even the angels were emotionally aroused in the crescendo of excitement just as I was every time Robert broke loose.

For the first time in almost three years there was a significant element missing at **Church of Living Waters**. I believe not only was it evident, but there were plenty of conversations of concern that afternoon at the lunch tables. *"I wonder what's going on. Did you notice Troy was sitting in the back? He didn't even stand during praise and worship."* I learned these were only a few of the questions asked by many who knew of my growing struggles.

Betty Jo danced across the stage. Her feet kicked back sharply as she seemed to glide effortlessly center stage and back to the Pastor seating. She always clapped and stepped with annunciation and perfect rhythm. I can remember countless Sunday afternoons we laughed as my younger sister would appear, in Mama's high heels, dancing, clapping and singing the very song Betty Jo danced to that Sunday morning. Michelle could mimic her perfectly. Gosh, those were the good Sunday afternoons. Even if there was the typical tension created by our step father, Michelle's theatrics were certain to bring our house to laughter.

The sounds were heavenly as the ladies harmonized and the voices of the congregation raised the ceiling with the repetitive angelic choirs. There were tears and shouts of praise. Once again, heaven had fallen, or emotion had elevated so those who participated felt heavenly. Betty Jo solemnly moved to center stage. The music continued while voices fell silent in anticipation. She took the microphone from the pedestal and said, *"Some of you young people listen to God tonight."* Her hand quivered with her voice as she pointed her finger through the congregation straight back at me. I was near the back row. *"T – R – O – Y, T – R – O – Y, TROY…God has a call on your life and you will never get out of it! Never, never, never, no matter what you do. No matter where you go, or how hard you try, you will never ever get out of the call God has on your life!"*

I don't recall much after these words. I just remember that I was not happy about God calling me out. I had a great deal of exposure to prophesy over the last seven years. I practiced some very unusual gifts at a young age. I knew when people were babbling their own ideas or simply just seeking the lime light. I also knew when I was in the presence of the "real deal." One thing I knew for certain was that Betty Joe Frank, she was the real deal. I knew Pastors Dr. Gene W. and Betty Jo, Gene Eldon, Darren and Keitha for more than seven years.

"Why would You tell her? How much does she know? I told You I was finished with all this! Leave me alone!"

My mind rattled the gates of heaven as I blushed in embarrassment. You see, until this service, I was ALWAYS on the second row with my hands raised high and my voice heard in unison with the Angels. I danced, clapped and shouted praise with the masses and perhaps more enthusiastically than most. Four days earlier, angry, heartbroken and very confused about life as I knew it, I cursed God. I was 15 years old, sitting in my bed room alone and I could not grasp how this was *"God's will."* Anger won the struggles my young mind wagered and at a whisper these words would shake the world.

"You know what God You can take this crap and shove it. I'll see You when I get there!"

The very next day I would purchase my first marijuana and by the weekend I tried cocaine. I now had a new life. The issues that seemed unbearable were no longer so significant. Although it was over two years before I experienced anything other than marijuana and alcohol again, I had broken the ice. It was okay to venture into the unknown of narcotics. This day marked **THE CHOICE**. My mind was resolved, and my heart determined. I would live my life on my own and I would prove to myself and everyone who knew me that I would succeed without *"God."* Notice God in quotes. My reference of *"God"* is as He had been imposed on me. My heart knew Him much different. Yet, my mind was overcome with anger and confusion. I had to discard the idea and any association with *"Him."* No longer could I be the young man sitting near the front row and joining in the celebrations of music and other church festivities. In fact, it would be impossible to drag me near any church gatherings. My choice abruptly disassociated me from anything that would attach me to *"God."* I am not exactly sure how to tell you I reached this decision. I can only share what I remember and where I ended up. I will share my opinions and perspective of each memory as we journey together to Truth, Redemption and Liberty. My hope and ambition are that you find yourself eagerly anticipating the next page and the new life of freedom destined through our discoveries.

I am convinced it was not a solitary event, a single word, an individual incident, or the impact of one person. No, I believe I have charted my voyage from a culmination of conceptions. I believe it is these conceptions that directed my choices and therefore my destinations. The beautiful gift is that no destination is final. We can reset our sail, choose a new course and create a new destiny.

There are times in which events occur and it seems there is no element of reason. It may also seem that there wasn't even a choice. Emotions grip our very existence and instinct overtakes any effort of reasoning. I am persuaded our environments sculpt our philosophies, thus world wrecking choices are sometimes made. *"Sometimes"* is my chosen term because in these exact same circumstances, right choices, miracles and destinies are determined of glorious treasure.

CHAPTER 4

I didn't know my biological father at fifteen. The man who gave us his last name solidified that nothing I did was good enough. Grandpa had disappeared almost two years prior. Conceptions of never being worthy, always begging for forgiveness and how *"God"* would chastise me for just being me, were overwhelming. There was absolutely nothing attractive about *"Christianity"*. I had to find acceptance somewhere. The result was devastating. My perception would crush my life. It would devastate hearts and minds of those my life touched. I expect I am not aware of many I hurt because of my ideas.

After the accident I decided to move back home to the ones I knew loved and accepted me no matter what, Mama and my two beautiful sisters, Dee Anne and Michelle. Although we had moved from Sealy, Texas, my fourth-grade year, our family was migrating back. My soon to be ex-wife and I had lived here in our last home together. We have roots and longtime family friends in Sealy. Mom had just recently married Papa T. who is more amazing than we could have ever prayed for Mama.

I was determined to achieve success and persuade my wife for another chance, but it did not happen. Every night, for about six months, I wrote to her through journal entries in a spiral notebook. This time I would not fail. I was determined, my mind was resolved, and I would *"get my life right with God!"* I was active in church, developing relationships with *"good Christians"* and was even speaking Christianese fluently. God had no choice but to answer my prayers and bless me. I was walking the walk, talking the talk and doing the deal just as prescribed.

Mama and I visited my kindergarten girlfriend's parents one afternoon shortly after I moved back to Sealy. They informed me that night was her 10-year class reunion. I decided to attend. Because of theater competitions in high school I had some reconnections. Mama is amazing at maintaining friendships so there were a few I would know and remember from our visits over the years.

It was a grand reunion and I reconnected with many I had not seen in 19 years. Wow! I didn't realize how much I would be remembered! Then it happened. I was approached by an outstretched hand. As customary, I reached and shook the man's hand with a smile introducing myself by name.

"You don't remember me, do you?" *"No sir, I can't say as I do."* I said reluctantly. He proceeded to remind me what great friends we were as fourth graders. We lived just down the road from one another and played almost every day. We chased rabbits with our BB guns, fished, tracked, had rock fights and other fun stuff country boys do.

"The day you were moving I brought you a gift and you beat me up." "Do what?" *"You're kidding?"* I responded embarrassed and with a shameful chuckle.

"Nope, and I never understood why you treated me that way. We were best friends." He exclaimed. My head fell in shame and I immediately apologized. How could I have discarded such an event? How could I have forgotten my best friend?

I cannot count the number of times we moved growing up, but this time was significant. Grandpa would no longer be just down the road. I would no longer see him, and he couldn't pull down the driveway on his way home or pick me up on the way to town. No longer would I hear his double horn he had custom installed as he passed. He could not stop by just to kiss me and say, *"Hi son."* I wouldn't be able to stay all the nights at the ranch with Grandpa, Grandma and Jeff. Jeff is my uncle but only two and a half months older than me. We were raised together and he's more like my brother. I was being taken away again. There was nothing I enjoyed more than being with Grandpa, Grandma and Jeff as I recall. Obviously, none of this was my best friend's fault, nor did he have any idea of my struggles. However, my perspective as a nine-year-old boy changed his world. Today I wonder how my choice may have caused him to hurt others. I also wonder how many others I discarded or hurt.

CHAPTER 5

It was a very exciting Saturday in the summer of 1973. We drove into the driveway all the way to the back near the screened porch. As we turned the corner off the main street, I looked across the beautiful plush, green St. Augustine grass. Massive oak trees shaded the yard and produced the leaf piles we grew up running, jumping, rolling and burying ourselves in every fall. The small two-bedroom house was surrounded with flower beds lined in Monkey grass. The perimeter fence lines and the two-story garage apartment were all lined with matching landscape.

GaGa, our great-grandmother, Gertrude Spangler, was given the name we called her by Mama, her only grandchild. GaGa (pronounced Gay Gay) was so beautiful. Her joy was expressed in the fabulous flower beds and immaculate lawn that filled our lives with so much joy and happiness. There was never a moment of sadness at GaGa's and PaPa's. This was heaven in our hearts and minds.

Gaga called me Foy-Foy. I got this name from my older sister who pronounced tr's as f's while developing her vocabulary. She is only 15 months older than me. You can only imagine the embarrassment Mama experienced when driving and Dee Anne would spot a truck.

With the excitement of a learning child, Dee Anne would exclaim *"Look Mama, a *..."* The pristine beautiful young lady who had not been raised around profanity was certain to blush and immediately attempt some sort of recovery for my sister.

GaGa loved flowers and typically had a childhood memory or story to share as she escorted us along the flower bed pointing out their beauty. Most amazingly she was certain to turn and express how much more beautiful we were than even the flowers. You can bet that she meant every word of her love. Although she's been in heaven almost 30 years I see her all the time. Mama expresses her love to me in so many ways it would take another book to share them all. I have told Dee Anne many, many times that she has GaGa's heart. Oh, and Michelle brings GaGa's smile and laughter to every room she enters. GaGa never left us. She lives in our hearts as real as she held our hands. Today, as we share memories of her and how she is missed, I think of the pansies. I hear her voice echoing in my heart, *"They turn their faces up to smile at the sun Foy Foy."* I smile because she left so much love with us all. My babies know her because we share her stories and her love as if she is still in the room with us. I can only hope that I too share a portion of GaGa with my family as they do with me.

I jumped out of the car and grabbed the 1972 Zenith green and white portable cassette recorder by its handle. It was cutting edge technology. The microphone was included and plugged in on the left side of the compact machine. It was approximately 12" long, 8" wide and 3" to 3 1/2" thick. There were six buttons in front, just behind the handle. Each button was about 1/2" wide by 1 1/2" long and remained down when depressed in place to introduce their function, except the stop and eject buttons. The stop button made the play, fast forward and rewind buttons pop up. The eject button did the same for the lid that housed the cassette, which was positioned in front of the single speaker. The cassette lid was transparent, so we could watch the cassette wind.

Mama had utilized our step-father's education and trade to create a lucrative income for our family. She became a Zenith representative and would later win a trip to Spain. **Bill William's TV and Appliances** had repair centers and showrooms in four locations. Anyway, I held the latest technology in portable recordable sound. O yeah, not only did it plug in but it also worked on batteries. If memory serves me correctly, it held six C batteries.

The car doors shut with a bang as I ran to beat Dee Anne and Michelle inside. GaGa was standing at the screen door waiting to hug and kiss each one of us. I quickly kissed her, but my hands were as full as my mind. I had my course plotted long before we arrived. Straight in the door I immediately slid to the carpet, reached behind the TV and plugged in the state-of-the-art player. I reached to the TV and turned it off. PaPa never questioned me but had moved forward in his chair anxiously waiting for his hug and kiss too. I popped up and went straight to his lap. PaPa tightly wrapped his arms around me, squeezed and waited for his kiss. *"PaPa, I brought a recording of our Sunday choir. Wait, when Mama comes in we're gonna listen to it. You'll love it. You can hear me singing really loud."*

We were born into the **Missouri Synod Lutheran Church**. All three of us were sprinkled, dedicated and had God-parents. We didn't miss a service, or a function and we made Mama proud with our Sunday school lessons, participation and recollection of what we learned.

When in the main service we were expected to participate and if there was anything but perfect behavior it was bent with a sharp pinch from Mama. One thing for certain, Mama was tough. She was not ashamed to expose our fannies in public and emboss them with a red impression of her hand if warranted. However, never has the world seen a more loving, caring and tender mother than ours. She is the very expression of the heart of GaGa and the Loving Kindness of God! Mama organized, assembled, and directed the children's choir. We practiced on most all our car travels and were more prepared than all participants. Mama inserted the cassette, closed the lid and depressed the play button. *"Shhh, listen."* I said. The quaint little living room fell silent and the Zenith player buzzed through its speaker. We heard little feet rustling and our young voices chatter. *"Shhh, get ready, one two three."* Mama's hands came down to direct our young voices in unison.

"Did you hear me; did you hear me?" I begged. *"Yes, Foy Foy, we all heard you",* GaGa said as a tear of joy ran down her cheek. I rushed to the recorder, mashed the stop button and clack, the play button popped up. I then mashed the rewind button all the way down, so it snapped in place. Whizzzz…the cassette raced back to the beginning and the rewind button popped up automatically.

"Shhh," I insisted as I depressed the play button again. I'm not sure how many times I did this until Mama insisted GaGa and PaPa had heard it enough. As they sat and talked we took off and played with all our familiar toys in every happy space of our own little heaven. It is of great importance that you understand that most of my childhood was exceptional. I know today that I experienced more love, tenderness and acceptance than most children could ever imagine. It is even of greater relevance to understand that I've always known Jesus. **"Yes, Jesus loves me"** was probably the first song I could sing. This is particularly important information for you in this journey. It is relevant to solidify that all my experiences, perspectives, ideas and positions are of one who is in Christ. I have no experience and therefore no personal truths of anyone outside of Christ. I cannot speak from the perspective of an unbeliever. Those of you who know me have heard me say, *"One thing I can tell you for certain is, I don't know – I was not there."*

I believe that no person really knows the perspective of another. We have not walked in their shoes, had their experiences, or lived from their perspective. I find it very difficult to say, *"I can't believe they would do that…"* or especially *"Can you believe that he…?"* These are bold yet common statements of judgment and arrogance. What I can say is *"I don't know, nor do I understand because I was not there."*

Later in life I would learn that GaGa was Catholic, at some point my Grandmother, NiNi, GaGa's only child became Lutheran and Mom was raised in a very stringent Lutheran belief. PaPa however had his own beliefs. The one I will never forget was pretty simple. It was respected and adhered to in his home. *"We don't talk about religion or politics."* These subjects were of opinion and therefore controversial. They were certain to create strife. There was never strife at GaGa and PaPa's. This is why it was the safest and most heavenly place my sisters and I knew. PaPa died around my 10th birthday and because of our personal relationship with Jesus, he too, dances in heaven with GaGa and NiNi.

I am in no hurry to join them and in hope it will be decades before anyone else meets up with them. Truth is I hold a personal distain for the philosophy of an anxious departure. I especially am discouraged by the pulpits that rant about the gloom of the world and the glory of getting out. Really?! Well, again, I do not know where they have been or what they have experienced, but I can only imagine they were not blessed with a GaGa who held their hand and pointed out the beauty of the flowers.

CHAPTER 6

On another beautiful Saturday morning, there was dew still on the ground and glistening like little stars dancing on the perfectly manicured St. Augustine grass. There was no place more wonderful than Grandma's yard on the **Boots and Saddle Ranch**. Grandma loved plants and what I remember most were her amazingly healthy, robust indoor plants. Beautiful large, medium and small plants were strategically placed downstairs in front of all the windows. Her personal secret to maintaining the most envied indoor plants you can possibly envision was Pearl beer. Along with the regimented daily dosage of water she popped a tab and poured the hops in the soil of each vibrant green plant.

We woke up and darted downstairs. Jeff and I went out the front door and jumped on our Big Wheels. We raced around Grandpa's Cadillac and his fully-loaded, wood grain, side-panel station wagon, underneath the large porta cache. We zipped past Grandma's brand- new metallic brown, 1974, four-door Cadillac Eldorado. This exquisite automobile had plush camel leather interior and a black convertible top.

The night before Jeff and I convinced Grandma to safety pin our large super hero beach towels to our necks and we played Batman and Robin for hours in the new Cadillac convertible. I am not certain if this was the weekend I trapped Jeff's neck between the front windshield frame and the huge convertible top or if that was one of our other fun-filled adventures, but Jeff and I ran freely enjoying every activity our creative minds could conceive. There was no end to the fun on the **Boots and Saddle Ranch**.

Grandpa custom designed and built the 7,800 square foot home on top of the largest point of the 296-acre ranch. There was a large horse shoe, pea-gravel driveway through the massive gable front porta cache and circling the beautiful swimming pool. We took off down one of the drives to the base where it met with the asphalt driveway. The drive was lined with oak trees all the way to the base of the hill. The one and a quarter mile drive took a 90-degree left turn and went past the 10,000 square foot barn adjacent to the three silos: big, bigger, and biggest. Trust me there wasn't a square foot of the ranch that Jeff and I didn't cover throughout our childhood. Yes, we climbed each silo's ladder inside and out. The driveway continued past the turn off that went to the top of the hill to the ranch hands' homes.

Just beyond the trophy house and stilt home was the front entrance with its large brick towers that matched Grandpa's house. A life-size Appaloosa horse was on the very top center-supported by a pipe that arched to each side of the entry. The entire ranch was pastured with eight-foot chain-link fence. The **Boots and Saddle Ranch** was amazing. There were award winning horses in every pasture. This was the home of world famous Wapiti Jr. and nationally renowned Jokers Wild. I assure you this was an absolute wonderland for young boys.

To the right of the houses' circle drive, along the eight-foot fence, was the third driveway that was three times as long as the other two. Although it was not as steep, there was still no way to keep our feet peddling the low profile speeding Big Wheels as we raced down. At the base of this driveway was some sort of construction with several pieces of 4' x 8' plywood and a couple of saw horses.

Jeff and I both liked Batman, Superman and Speed Racer but our favorite of superheroes were the real live ones. At the top of the chart was Evil Knievel. We had every figurine, miniature motorcycle and the modular action figure ramps. When these set ups were not enough, Grandma's album collection, books and decorative throw pillows provided the structure needed for our obstacle course. The massive slick kitchen floor was covered with our oversized ramps. Our Evil Knievel motorcycle raced from one end to the other and made death defying jumps that Evil himself would have envied.

"Okay, you grab that side and I'll get this one." Jeff instructed. We moved the saw horses over to line them up to the end of the long driveway. We then strategically placed the heavy plywood on the saw horses, approximately four to five feet past where the pea gravel met the asphalt. We would hit the first piece at its four-foot side that touched the asphalt. It was only eight feet to the top of the plywood leaning against the first sawhorse. Our plan was for me to land in between the two and launch off the second ramp only twenty-five or thirty feet away. Our kitchen course had nothing on the Big Wheel Evil Knievel set up we constructed.

Atop the one eighth mile drive was a long six car garage where Grandpa kept his 1960 Silver Cloud Rolls Royce with original right- hand steering. Jeff and I pushed our Big Wheels to the top where the driveway levelled out across the entire front of the garage. He explained how I would go first and coached me on the required techniques to launch and land successfully. I was always first when it came to any of our grave, dare devil stunts. Jeff and I could write an entire book on our amazing, dangerous and adventurous childhood on the **Boots and Saddle Ranch**. When together, we still tell these stories and laugh uncontrollably as listeners' awe, gasp and laugh with us.

"Okay, make sure you are in the center of the ramp. Hold your feet up when you land in between and don't miss the second ramp. I'll come down as soon as you land the second jump."

My heart was beating with excitement as Jeff gave me the countdown to launch. I gripped the handlebars and twisted the right- hand grip to rev the engine as if it were a real motorcycle. Our feet were covered with a pair of

Grandpa's brand-new black silk socks. We had unpackaged them before we went out the front door, sat on the steps and pulled the large black socks up to our knees. We imagined they were the boots Evil himself laced up before his performance. We were dressed in our Fruit of the Loom white underwear for our morning of adventure and fun. This was our typical pre-lunch Saturday attire at Grandpa's and Grandma's.

"Three, two, one, POW!" Jeff shouted as I peddled my sleek racing machine. This was the greatest test of endurance our machines had seen thus far. They were worn and scared from many adventures and stunts, but none had rivaled this Saturday morning flight. I could not have been a fourth of the way down and the big front wheel turned much faster than I could peddle. I lifted my feet and watched the wheel spin faster and faster. In just seconds it spun so fast it was nothing but a blur. In my six-year-old imagination my hair was pushed straight back, cheeks flapping from the G forces and the tassels on my sleeves popped as they slapped my arms. About two-thirds down the driveway, just like Superman, I became fully outfitted in my imaginary Evil Knievel suit. *Yaaaa!!!!* At Mach one I became airborne. With my knees locked and legs stretched straight out I looked left to the fence line. I soared higher than the eight-foot chain link fence. Quickly my head snapped, I looked down as I cleared the second ramp. I gasped, realizing the fence veered right and there was no steering my cycle in full flight. I landed with a thud just in front of the six-foot stretch of grass that lined the fence perimeter. My only hope to bring my stunt cycle to a stop was my *Fred Flintstone* emergency brakes. My feet pressed down and ripped the bottoms out of the brand-new pair of Grandpa's silk socks. I can assure you Jeff did NOT follow my lead.

Although I was ecstatic, there was a look of amazement and trembling fear in Jeff's eyes. This stunt did not go as planned but it seared an indelible mark of heroic fun in our childhood history on the **Boots and Saddle Ranch.**

Jeff and I were so thrilled about our accomplishment our joy alerted the livestock from pasture to pasture. It was as if they all celebrated our fantastic feat with us. This jump was certain to be printed in The Guinness Book of World Records, if only we had it recorded somewhere other than our memories.

CHAPTER 7

We ran across the still damp yard, leaped through the flower beds and met Grandma at the front door. Her hands were clinched to her cheeks and her eyes as wide as silver dollars. She ran from the dining room out the front door after witnessing *The World Record Setting Big Wheel Jump.* You can believe that she was always somewhere near, making sure she could rescue us when our imagination got out of control. Jeff and I jumped up and down shouting our own views of this amazing Evil Knievel stunt simultaneously. Grandma broke down in her beautiful laughter as she examined there were no physical injuries. Grandpa came out the front door and joined in the celebration. They even laughed as they saw the condition of the brand-new silk socks.

The story Grandma always enjoyed telling of our death-defying adventures was slightly more dangerous. Fortunately, she caught us before we had started the count down. Grandpa, in his up and coming days, was an underwater welder. We enjoyed many stories growing up of his underwater feats. Our imaginations soared as we became advanced swimmers at a young age with front door access to the swimming pool. Grandpa even had a large heated cover that engulfed the entire pool area for the winters.

Anyway, Jeff and I searched the premises looking for just the right bricks and rocks that would stack properly in my back pack. We zipped the pack and wrestled it toward the swimming pool. I think we set it down three or four times prior to reaching the pool side of the deep end. We then ran to the flower bed and drug out the garden hose, placing it next to the back pack. In full stride we ran to change into our swim suits. I imagine in our typical excitement we discussed the particulars of the necessary techniques and strategies we should use to accomplish our grave dare-devil underwater adventure. Once again Jeff coached me in how it would be necessary for me to go first and once successfully completed he would follow suit. Our clothes were flying off as we raced to Jeff's room. Faster than greased lightning we were in our swimsuits and poolside. Little did we know our Guardian Angel, Grandma, had been listening in and was directly behind us. Even though this death-defying feat also created an indelible mark in the history of the **Boots and Saddle Ranch** adventures, it never launched. Although frantic, Grandma was very gracious as she explained my certain death from depending on oxygen from the twenty-five-foot garden hose. As a duo we must have kept Grandma on pins and needles.

Grandpa: T.J. Bryant Sr., *Thomas Jefferson*, also known as *Whitey*, was an amazing man with history making accomplishments. Houston's ship channel and water ways throughout Texas to this day are marked with his soul print. Swing gate bridges that he designed on notebook paper, while sitting on the toilet, still operate in Port Isabel and Sargent, Texas. The one built from his pencil sketch in Freeport, Texas, has been removed and replaced with a large bridge. Grandpa was filled with loving grace and tenderness. He was much more Daddy than Grandpa to me and my sisters. I named my son after him.

This particular summer was even more special than most. Grandpa had planned a spectacular event for the eldest grandchildren and Jeff. We enjoyed a fun-filled week at Camp J Bar J on I-10 just west of the Brazos River. The required age was seven. I would not be seven until September 20th, but Jeff's birthday is July 4th. Stacey and Dee Anne were both nine years old. Grandpa made special arrangements for me to go at only six years of age. Grandpa had a way of making special provisions for us no matter where we were or what we were doing.

When I was about 14 years old Dee Anne, Michelle and I visited him in Acapulco, Mexico. The real *Love Boat, The Pacific Princess,* was at port and the passengers were touring Acapulco. Knowing we had grown up watching the television series with Mama, Grandpa escorted us to the bridge entrance and explained to the crew attendant, who guarded its entrance from non-ticket holders, how we would be entering the ship, so he could show us it's interior. I remember he shared how we loved the TV show. No different than any other event, Grandpa explained how we would be doing exactly what was prohibited! We entered the ship with hospitable acceptance and enjoyed our own private tour, escorted by Grandpa. Camp was amazing! There was an old cowboy town setting, swimming for coins tossed in the pool, horseback riding, water skiing, canoeing, paddle boat races, sailing, dancing and a talent show. Wow! What a summer we experienced. Grandpa was so pleased from our joy and excitement we went back the following summer.

Our third summer camp experience changed destinations as we ventured a little further from home. We would not hear the double freight train horn as Grandpa passed on his way home, nor would we enjoy his visit and midweek kiss. This adventure would take us west to a Lutheran Camp near LaGrange, Texas. There was campfire singing and even a nightly bible lesson. We were privileged with a young male counselor who played the guitar and glowed with a joyful presence I found very alluring. One evening later in the week he handpicked a group of us to follow him on a hike. The sun set as we found our campsite destination up the hill. He played and sang the songs we learned after several days of camp. As the campfire crackled, he slowly strummed his guitar and talked about a real relationship with Jesus. He explained how he had asked Jesus to live in his heart. I reasoned that if this was his evident joyous difference, and if it's available to me, then I wanted it. Beneath the magnificent constellations, nestled amongst the trees and gathered around the campfire, I too asked Jesus to live in my heart. I was 8 years old. This was a world changing decision. It was certain to radically change our family's voyage.

CHAPTER 8

"Don't take my word for it, check it out for yourself." The pastor of **The Shepherd's Way Church** in Sealy, Texas, Frank Lucas dogmatically insisted. These words became some of my very favorite as I enjoyed listening to him Sunday after Sunday, 1997 through 2001.

My wife and I visited with Mama before things fell apart and I moved to Dallas for employment. Mostly I took the geographical relocation as another grasp for hope. Hope that I could stay sober. Countless personal attempts and a plethora of broken promises stole our love. I meant every one of them, with all my heart, determination and resolve. I have relived every disappointment I created and every promise I ever broke, over and over. There is not one ounce of my existence that hasn't screamed in anguish, bellowed in regret, wailed for forgiveness and begged for a means to make it right. It took me over 10 years before I began to forgive myself for the life I put her through. It is now 20 years later, and I occasionally struggle with the *woulda, coulda, shouldas*. Fact is I have shed tears while writing and remembering her beauty. Not all of my tears have been of sorrow or regret, because there were many wonderful memories of joy, laughter and love. The truth is I honestly did not know or understand the value of what we shared. I had no concept of the power and strength of marriage. I mostly did not know how to cherish love. I think she knew how and I believe she hurt on my behalf knowing the real me who was running and hiding.

She flew to Dallas for her last visit the first weekend in February 1997. We had an amazing weekend. We toured Dallas and Ft. Worth, dined out, laughed, held hands and gazed in one another's eyes. I had amazing hope for this next geographical relocation. The weekend was over, and her flight left Sunday morning. I took her to the American Eagle gate and we said our goodbyes. The look on her beautiful face will forever remain seared in my heart. Today I am of the opinion her tears of sorrow were because she knew we had experienced the last of our love. My endless reflection has persuaded me that her heart quivered in the struggles of knowing our union's end. My God, if only I had known!

I was certain to not miss church. I had my own personal designated spot on the front row. I was directly in front of my grandmother, NiNi *(Juanita Frances Bryant*, Mama's mother). Although my family knew I was broken, their hearts were warmed by my presence in church every Sunday. My voice was heard with the angels and my off-rhythm clap rattled the pearly gates. Caught in the whirlwind of emotional crescendos, with hands stretched high, there were innumerable tears that streaked my face most every service. I find it impossible to express the sincerity of my outcry to heaven. After 15 years I wasn't confident God would have much to do with me and certainly would not grace me with the same opportunities He did from age 9 to 13.

However, I desperately sought forgiveness and acceptance. I sought fortitude and strength to do what was necessary to succeed. In a very short time I had organized a men's prayer group. We met every Sunday morning prior to the service and once a week at a local café for breakfast. My name had become a buzz and there were requests for my participation in one activity after another. However, I could not stay sober. Although I kept the reigns tight, the beast of addiction always seemed certain to win.

Once again, I swore off any indulgences and dove deeper into being all I could be and doing all I could do to *"get right with God."* I promised God everything any person could possibly promise Him if He would just grant me His forgiveness and acceptance. There had not been a day that passed I did not journal to my soon to be ex-wife. I even wrote a poem begging for just one more chance. I mailed copies addressed to every one of her relatives I knew. I visited the court house where our divorce would be finalized and pinned copies on every floor. I placed them down the stairways and trapped them under the wipers of every car in the employee parking lot. This was my last-ditch effort to strong arm God into acting on my behalf. I read my Bible daily, watched at least 3 tele-evangelists every morning, spoke fluent Christianeeze and was giving 15% above my tithe. I had multiple Christian community activities under my belt, was a fixture at my home church and was certain to have a new guest at least one service a month. I absolutely was doing everything possible to ensure God would bless me. I was perfectly positioned for God to grant my saving grace.

I sat next to her in the courtroom and greeted her gracefully. We spoke kindly to one another. There were not many words exchanged before the room echoed with *"All rise."* When the judge called her to the front I stood as she was granted the divorce she requested, and I paid to execute. The judge opened the file and the gold paper the poem was printed on lay on top of the decree. There is one thing I am more certain of than anything else concerning our end. She knew then, and knows eternally, that I was deeply and honestly sorry for failing her and that I most assuredly loved her desperately. Even now I cry as I recall how beautiful she looked June 2, 1997. Trust me I can describe in perfect detail the pale aqua dress, her petite jewelry, dainty sandals and amazing smile. This was the very last time I saw her in person.

CHAPTER 9

Returning from camp, after Jesus filled my heart, I burst through the door *"Mama, Mama,"* I yelled as I ran in the kitchen and darted toward her with arms wide open. *"We had so much fun, and Camp was awesome!"* Uncle Tommy and Aunt Sandy had picked us up and dropped Dee Anne, Michelle and I off at our home just a couple of miles from the **Boots and Saddle Ranch**. We spent the rest of the afternoon telling Mama of all the wonderful fun we had at camp. We talked about Capture the Flag, hiking and jumping from the bridge into the Colorado River. Mostly, we shared about our new relationship with Jesus. We boasted about how He lived in our hearts and how God loves us, no matter what we've done wrong. She knew we could not possibly return to the **Missouri Synod Lutheran Church**. Mama knew her babies. She knew this was a sincere and real-life changing event. She also knew there would be nothing to prevent me sharing with everyone about Jesus.

Sunday morning several weeks later, we dressed our very best for church. We hustled out the house and rustled into our family car. I don't recall us ever being anything but early to church. The gravel tinged and clinked against the wheel wells as it was lifted from our drive and bounced off our avocado green Chevrolet station wagon. It was only about 18 miles from our home to the next town south of Sealy, Texas. Wallis is a fraction of the size of Sealy and so was the church as it was a small-town church built with white horizontal wood siding and wooden floors that creaked. My first impression this Sunday morning was the cute girl in the yellow dress with hair white as cotton and sparkling blue eyes. Next was the guy in Sunday school who had the same color hair and eyes. He shot me with rubber bands. I quickly learned both were the pastor's children. This was the first church we attended that had a children's church. We were not required to sit through the adult service. Our children's service was excused slightly before the adults and this permitted me the privilege of attempting to catch the pretty cotton haired girl in the yellow dress.

A new event occurred this Sunday we were not accustomed to. We returned to church Sunday evening. This service required attendance with the adults. My eyes were riveted on the pastor and not one word passed my ears. He was captivating even for a young child. For the first time in a church service I was not alerted with a pinch to harness my behavior. Pastor Gene Frank of the **Wallis Baptist Church** fascinated me. He possessed an even greater passion for Jesus than the counselor at camp. From this point forward, I had a particular gift to retain the messages and could recite them almost verbatim.

Sometimes it occurred in the middle of adults' conversations as they discussed the message and I quickly inserted the correct words if their conversation deviated from what was said. It soon became common for adults to quiz me after services about the word spoken by the pastor or evangelist. Mama became very active in women's functions and church activities. She relentlessly searched for Truth and where we fit in. We quickly became great friends with the pastor and family of the local **Assembly of God Church**. Miss Joyce played the piano amazing. She sang more beautiful than an angel and was always so pretty and sweet. She made special effort to ensure we all knew we were loved and welcome. Instantly we all felt comforted by her smile and gracious hospitality, whether at their home or church. Pastor Clyde Drake spoke with vehement passion and was certain to maintain my undivided attention during every service. It was here Miss Joyce introduced me to the joy of sitting on the front row. **Sealy Assembly of God** met in an old building downtown that was always filled beyond its maximum capacity.

"Come here darling, you sit right here sweetheart. I want you right here by Mama Joyce, precious." Wow, it was always as if I was the only person in the whole world. She sang straight to my heart and drew me in to my own heavenly experience. Even today I feel the same warmth and love when I am fortunate enough to visit their home.

CHAPTER 10

Ping tack ting tock tick tick tick – eeerrcck. Dust whirled through the air and it was difficult to see NiNi's car through the cloud. Her tires could be heard as the rubber met the asphalt the gravel flew in the air. She sped out in a rage of anger and disbelief. I can't imagine how Mama felt as the result of this response from her mother. Could it really mean that much? How could leaving a denomination create so much resentment and animosity? I learned later in life that NiNi wasn't the only person who viewed our church move with negativity. Mama revealed she was told by our Lutheran friends that her decision was not only wrong, but it reserved a first-class ticket to Hell for our entire family. I have read many of Martin Luther's writings. Rest assured this opinion in no way reflects his position or beliefs. I am more apt to consider that he would have made the exact same move. Amazing, this is almost identical to what Martin experienced himself by the Vatican. He was ridiculed, condemned and ostracized. Those whom he considered his Christian friends rejected him. This would be my first exposure to the judgment, ridicule and rejection by Christian friends. This, by NO MEANS, would be the last or the most detrimental.

Maybe you too have experienced surprising disappointments by *"Christians"* you whole heartedly trusted. Here I pose a simple question. Why? What is it that creates the philosophy in *"Christianity"* that it is right to judge, ridicule, condemn, reject and ostracize others? Why is it so easily justified? How is it done with such zeal and passion? There is NO where we find this in the heart of God. It is the antithesis of God's nature. It is anti-Christ not Christian.

Understand my use of the term anti-Christ. I am referring to ideas, concepts, ways of thinking, believing and behaving that oppose love. I believe this is the philosophy that the author of Hebrews calls an evil conscience. He is very specific in clarifying that doing right; speaking right, dressing right, acting right or any other effort to *"get right"* cannot rid one of this wrong thinking. Only a personal encounter with God's goodness and His infrangible love will dissolve our whickered conceptions.

CHAPTER 11

Summer of 1975 we traveled I-10 West toward the state line. *"Mama, where are we now? Are we still in Texas?" "Yes, baby, we are still in Texas." "How big is Texas?"*

I volunteered to keep Mama awake as we drove in our dark green Chevy 1/2-ton pick-up truck through the night. The truck seemed to sway and rock from side to side. The week prior was full of excitement preparing for our journey. The camper that would set in the bed of our truck was in the backyard. It was on jack stands and a small step stool was used to climb inside. The restroom was on the left with its tiny toilet, sink and shower combo. A stove top and a half pint refrigerator were on the right. There was a small table with benches that converted to a bed. The best part of our cool miniature house was the bed that stuck out over the top of the pick-up truck cab. It had windows across the front where we spent much of our trip laying shoulder to shoulder while looking past the hood of the truck. Mama planned many stops along the way to our Las Vegas destination. The night seemed long because problems with the camper tail lights caused significant delays, and getting our entire crew loaded was a tedious chore itself. This 1,425-mile journey from Sealy, Texas, to Las Vegas, Nevada, would take three days. **Disney Land**, in Anaheim, California, would finalize our West bound journey. This trip included me, Dee Anne, Michelle, Mama, Bill Williams; our step-Dad who adopted us all, his youngest on Shane and our childhood babysitter, Kim Janzen. Kim was 16, Shane 13, Dee Anne 10, Michelle 6 and I was almost 9.

"Mama is Texas really this big? I'm a good helper, right? I've helped you stay awake, right Mama?" I imagine I wasn't awake any longer than it took me to run through all my 8-year-old questions. There is nothing in life more comforting than being with Mama. I still have the exact feeling today.

"Wow! Look at all the different colors of dirt, this is so cool. It's huge!" We could see all the way across the **Grand Canyon**. We pulled into a parking area and walked to a lookout point which had a telescope that required a dime. In the bottom of the **Grand Canyon** was the river that appeared as small as the miniature ones I dug for my match box cars at home. It was such a magnificent sight! It's now been over 40 years and its beauty remains in my mind today just as it was from the afore-mentioned point. Mama quickly hustled us back in the camper, so we might reach our next destination before night fall. Arriving, she rousted us all out and over to an "X" painted on the ground.

"Kim, you and Michelle stand here, Dee Anne you stand here, Troy over there and Shane you stand right there." Mama instructed then explained how each one of us was standing in a different state. *"All four states join at corners right here."*

Mama explained how no other place is like this and how unique it is to every other adjoining line on the map of the USA. She took our picture then once again hustled us back into the camper. We continued our journey in adherence to her tight schedule. *"Where are we going next Mama?"* Dee Anne asked as she held the Polaroid watching the picture magically appeared. *"Look, look. I'm in Colorado, Kim and Michelle are in Utah, Troy you are in New Mexico and Shane is in Arizona."* *"I wanna see."* Michelle exclaimed as she darted under Dee Anne's arms and reached for the fully developed photo.

It was dusk and no matter how fast we moved, we couldn't catch the Sun. Kim prepared dinner and we played checkers and cards as our cottage continued westward to **Las Vegas**.

CHAPTER 12

For many months before we left to go to **Vegas** we practiced Black Jack. *"Hit me."* I had the ace of spades and the two of hearts. I learned that this hand could be 13 or 3. The object was to get 21. If I went over then I busted. *"I'll stand."* I was dealt the six of clubs. Nineteen was a good hand and I didn't have to make the ace a one. I only had to beat the dealer to win, and with a king showing he could likely bust.

Every night Bill, whom we called Dad, would have us gather at the table to play. He practiced the strategies he read about in several books and was determined to become a professional Black Jack gambler. So, our trip to **Las Vegas** was said to be the first of many in our future. We played with a minimum of three decks and he instructed us in each new strategy. Counting cards was a bit more than we could grasp, but playing Black Jack beat the heck out of being scolded over making too much noise. His practice did not exclude the pastors, evangelists and church friends. Although our circle of new church friends didn't consider Black Jack to be approved by God, they graciously entertained the invitation.

"Come on kids, get out. This is Hoover Dam! It is the largest dam in the world. The dam was created to hold water, so the entire desert could have a water supply." We awed as we peered over the rail. The endless expanse beyond the dam is an amazing sight! We took turns looking through the telescopes that also required a dime. *"Next stop Las Vegas!"* We all cheered and loaded into the camper. This time every one of us went straight for the big overhead bed so we could view the spectacular scenery as we crossed **Hoover Dam**. It was just after dusk as we came over the crest in view of the massive desert.

There were more colored lights than I had ever seen in my exceptional eight-year-old imagination. We pulled into the **Stardust Hotel** after passing **Circus Circus**, **The Sands**, **The Flamingo**, **MGM** and many bright lights. Mama and Bill got a room in the hotel and parked our camper truck in the **Stardust RV Park**. Our access to the hotel swimming pool and grounds along with the park's shower house, laundry room, and of course playground was awesome. We were in paradise. We went to **Circus Circus** almost every night. This turned out to be one of our most memorable family vacations. After more than a week of fun in fabulous **Las Vegas**, we traveled to our final vacation destination, **Disneyland**.

We stayed an additional night beyond our schedule to attend church Sunday morning in **Las Vegas**. *"Mama, what's that book you're reading? You've been reading it the whole trip."* My inquisitiveness was cut off when the huge band and choir began to play. This was the most enormous church I had ever seen. Not only was it huge, but it looked far more like an arena compared to all the churches we ever visited. *"The book is called 'They Spoke* *with Other Tongues', son. Now shhh, church is starting."* Although Mama was always serious about us behaving in church there was something significantly different about her ambition to silence me. She didn't seem pressed about others hearing us. I was certain she was serious about hearing everything this service offered.

CHAPTER 13

Returning home from vacation, Mama put me in charge of directing traffic. I stood near the end of our driveway as one car after the other turned in. Each car following the last parked along the edge of our long dirt driveway. We spent hours cleaning the house, rearranging the living room and setting up chairs. This became a common Saturday night function at our home.

Mama has a baby grand piano Grandpa bought for her on her 6th birthday in **New York**. The elegant baby grand and the master piece painting of Mama as **Kendall County Queen 1963** were central themes of décor no matter where we lived, and they still are today. Dee Anne, Michelle and I all have beautifully framed prints of the painting. It is one of my favorite treasures and ranks at the top of any Christmas gift I ever received.

There was the familiar sound of what became common church choruses and things occurred here that never occurred in any church service where I attended. About 100 people filled our large living room of the home custom built just as Mama had designed. Almost every person in the room was standing with hands stretched high, eyes closed and singing. However, each person sang a different song. It was angelic, heavenly and amazing. I couldn't understand any of the words they were singing. No one sang the same words, the same melody or the same rhythm but it was perfect and harmonious. They had not practiced and most of the guests didn't seem to know one another. The music we heard rivaled any Beethoven master piece.

There was no conductor, no harmony missing and no one off key. Then, as suddenly as it began, it stopped. Without a queue or a prompt, a man began to speak from the center of the room. He spoke assertively, with great diction and annunciation. However, he spoke in a language I did not know. Almost as soon as he finished a man in the front of the room took over. This man spoke in English and I understood it. He used the same rhythm and annunciation as the previous man did. I was mesmerized by what was transpiring. I still remember tears dripping from my cheeks. I don't recall why, I merely recall that something significant occurred in my heart.

"I was 19 years old and pronounced dead at the scene" announced the guest speaker. Evangelist Gary Wood talked about his death and his visit to Heaven in specific detail. He described magnificent splendor beyond the pearly gates. The people lined up and Gary placed his hands on their heads and prayed. He too spoke to them in a language I didn't understand. It was different than what any others spoke. Then one after the other they fell

30

over. Our living room had people lying on the floor everywhere. I never witnessed this before, but for some reason it seemed perfectly okay.

More than three hours passed, and the room was still full. Everyone stuck around, huddled in circles and talked about their personal experiences with God. Mama sent us down the hall and instructed us to go to bed. After brushing my teeth and dressing in my pajamas, I negotiated my way back toward the guests. The group had become much smaller and was gathered in the kitchen area.

Our kitchen and dining area were 32' foot long and 14' foot wide. The cabinets were custom built on site, including the all wood lazy Susan. There was plenty of room for the gathering and Mama was an excellent hostess. There was something very unique and alluring about the guests that remained. Mr. Gary and Mr. Lamar Thomas talked to Dad about their pastor while Miss Deena and Miss Carolyn talked about the wonderful miracles they too witnessed at their church. Mama asked what we thought about visiting. The answer was instantaneous. Despite our excitement she insisted we hustle back to our rooms and in our beds pronto. *"Yes, Ma'am"* we replied as we darted to our rooms. We are still friends with Deena, Angel and David, Mr. Lamar and Carolyn Thomas.

CHAPTER 14

Summer of 1997, I was shattered by divorce. *"I Need You More"* by Lindell Cooley had become my favorite song.

"I need you more More than yesterday I need you more
More than words can say….."

The small praise and worship team was spectacular at **The Shepherd's Way**. Brother Frank taught another riveting message and as always, he insisted he was merely reading the Word. *"I'm just reading it. Check it out for yourself. I want you to study the Word for yourself!"* I took these words to heart. I was certain I didn't want to trust the opinions, ideas or concepts of others. I wanted to see and understand God for myself.

Typically, after each service I hung around to visit. I meandered toward the exit where I saw Papa T talking with a couple of ladies. A young attractive lady spoke well and had a Southern Bell dialect that caught my immediate attention. Unfortunately, I was called to assist Mama and could not introduce myself.

Things were looking up. My new business was building rapidly, and my mind had settled down. I put together a few months of sobriety and the sting of divorce was replaced with anxious anticipation of a miraculous reconciliation. I was convinced God had no option but to perform this miracle on my behalf. The divorce was final but I remained faithful.

"God was just testing my faith." This was just one of the clichés of encouragement I was given. I still searched every method of Christianology. I did not want to leave one stone unturned. I needed absolutes. I sought direction from the most spiritual. I made certain I attended services across Houston featuring the big names. I followed prophets and jockeyed seating to be in clear sight. I hung out with the finest of *"Christians"* and begged silently for any of them to assure me I had captured God's attention.

One Saturday evening watching TV at Mama's house I nearly jumped out of my skin with excitement. *"It's T.D. Jakes. He's in Dallas. His church is called **The Potter's House***" Mama explained. He pierced my heart with the love and acceptance the Prodigal Son received. I pondered his emphasis on the father and not the son. He reiterated that the father stood waiting everyday his son was away, and how he was thrilled when his son returned. I don't recall that Bishop Jakes ever mentioned how wrong the son was or that he was only accepted because he groveled. However, he said that the father paid no attention to the son's plea for forgiveness. He immediately orchestrated a celebration. Why didn't I believe this was true concerning me?

Mama asked if I would help prepare the dishes for the Sunday luncheon after church. *"Well, of course, I'd love to,"* I replied as she directed my assistance. To this day the kitchen is a comforting environment for me. I love to cook. It's one of my greatest passions and there is nothing more wonderful than cooking with Mama, Dee Anne and Michelle. At any given family event I can be found in the kitchen with the ladies. The only missing element in the best of life's moments is GaGa.

After church we caravanned to the local civic center where we enjoyed food, fun and fellowship. I hadn't been there very long when I heard that sweet Southern Bell voice that caught my attention just the week before. It took me a fraction of a second to pin point her position and make my way her direction. She stood talking with one hand on her hip, her ankles crossed, right foot forward and poised on the toe of her dainty high heel shoe. I positioned myself close so as to join in their conversation. She glanced my way, ended her sentence and smiled a cute little smile with a slight twist to her right cheek that held an enticing dimple. I capitalized on the pause and said, *"Hi, my name is …."* and before I could complete my flirtatious introduction she piped out, *"I know who you are Troy. "Really?"* I asked surprised. It didn't take but a short while and I had acquired Carol's phone number. After our flattering conversation I seemed to almost float away. Throughout the week we chatted over the phone and planned to spend the afternoon together the following Sunday, but not before I asked her to dinner Friday night.

A couple of days prior I made an intentional trip into Houston to the restaurant where we would dine. It was a small, quaint Thai restaurant I frequented a few years prior. I was on a first name bases with the owner.

"Hi Benzi, how have you been." I asked. *"Mr. Troy, I have not seen you in long time,"* he responded in his broken accent. *"Yes, I moved to Dallas for a while."* I reached into my front right pocket as I explained I recently divorced and would be bringing in a young lady whom I wanted to impress. *"Oh, yes, Mr. Troy, I will have nice dinner for you."* Benzi replied. *"I have also invited another couple so please prepare for all of us."* Mr. Benzi replied in his typical polite manner and smiled as I handed him two crisp $20.00 bills. Nothing else needed to be said. I knew Mr. Benzi would take care of all the details.

Friday could not come soon enough. I was certain to make an exceptional impression. We met my friend and his new wife at Benzi's place. I was greeted by name at the door as the hostess looked past several couples who waited for their tables.

"Hi, Mr. Troy, we have your table waiting. Follow me please." The hostess said while pointing to the table. We were escorted to a table positioned on a small platform along the back wall. It was the focal point of the floor plan and was the only preset table awaiting its distinguished guests. We were almost finished with our entrees when Carol said, *"They never even brought us menus."*

Benzi started us with an amazing shrimp soup then a couple of fantastic appetizers. The waiter, waitress and Benzi never missed a beat and neither did our conversations. The service was impressive, and we were treated like royalty. Benzi stood beside me after our table was cleared. I said *"Thank you Mr. Benzi. Dinner was amazing as usual."* *"Mr. Troy is customer my first day open here. He is a very good customer for a long time. Mr. Troy has special guest, so I make special dinner for him."* Benzi explained. I expressed how I stopped by and requested that Benzi make the night special. I told Mr. Benzi I never wanted to see a menu and asked him to serve what he thought best for our date.

"Mr. Benzi, two of the entrees I don't recall ever seeing on your menu." He immediately shared they were not and gave an exquisite description of their preparation. Then he continued by sharing how the wine was special from his personal selections. He described the desert and said it also was never on the menu. *"This one too difficult for normal guest, Mr. Troy."*

"Good night Carol." I said as I kissed her on the cheek and headed home. I had spent a couple of hours at her apartment continuing our wonderful evening. Conversation and laughter were all I intended for our first date. Call me a gentleman, a romantic or a Prince Charming and maybe I slightly suit all descriptions, but not one was my motive. No, I had to *"please God."*

CHAPTER 15

The following Sunday after church we went to lunch at a local Mexican food restaurant. It still ranks as one of my favorite Mexican food dining spots today. It's a small place facing the tracks in an old building in downtown Sealy that lacks elegance and authentic décor. It may be categorized by some as a dive. As customary lunch was with a group from church. I had managed to persuade Carol to take an afternoon country drive and she advised it was first necessary to go home and change into something more suitable for the country. *"Hey, Mama, may I borrow your Miata?"* Mama had a white Mazda Miata with a black convertible top she drove on special occasions. *"No, son,"* she replied. My jaw almost hit the floor. *"Ma'am"* I queried. *"No. Why do you need to use my car?"*

"Mom, I don't need to, I would like to for an evening drive through the country."

"Are you trying to impress that girl?"

"I'm not certain how I could do that. I'll be thirty years old this month, I have nothing and right now I'm living with my parents. You have never denied me driving any of your cars. What's wrong?" I asked.

"I don't know, I just don't think you should drive my car." Mama exclaimed as she handed me the keys. *"Thank you, Mama. I'll be careful." "Okay, son, I love you."* I leaned forward and kissed Mama the way I always have and still do today. *"I love you too."*

I exited out the back door and dashed over to the small two door sports car. The parking lights flashed, door locks clicked open and I heard chirp, chirp. Opening the door with my left hand and stepping into the car with my right foot, I slid into its low-profile sport seat. I then reached for the convertible's latch on the passenger side. More powerful, amazing, complex and astonishing than any creation in the entire universe is the human mind. It is capable of storing and retrieving experiences we are not even aware we remember. Instantly as my hand grasped the latch, I drifted back to childhood memories.

Mama had purchased the beautiful 1969 metallic blue, two-door Cadillac Eldorado from Grandpa. She had parked it behind our small retail appliance store. This particular location occupied a space between Mr. Aaron's liquor store and the hometown pharmacy. I scatted to the back alley and climbed in the big two door machine that simultaneously transformed into the Bat Mobile. I pushed the buttons on the radio, pulled the knobs and held onto the steering wheel as I raced out of the Bat Cave to Gotham City. I ran across the big white leather bench seat and unlatched the convertible top, first the passenger side then the drivers. Repositioning myself behind the steering wheel, I reached to the left and held the electric switch in the upward position until the top was fully collapsed. Fast as lightning, and without a thought, my left hand hit the two switches positioned in a cluster on the arm rest of the door panel that electronically rolled the door windows down. Then the two rear vent windows followed with the shifting of my fingers to the buttons behind the first two I had depressed. *"To the rescue,"* I shouted as I leaped over the door and to the ground. At full speed I darted down the alley. *"Pow, Wham, Pop..."* I took out the bad guys with swift and precise punches. I then darted back to the Bat Mobile.

This was my time to play Batman. I was always Robin on the **Boots and Saddle Ranch** when playing with Jeff. I jumped and pulled myself back over the door. I rustled around and maneuvered back to the pilot's position. Then quickly, I repeated all the same motions but in perfect reverse order. I returned the Bat Mobile to the Bat Cave.

However, I had forgotten one important step.

CHAPTER 16

I remember a particular Sunday morning around the fall of 1976. *"Hurry brush your teeth really good and get dressed. Your clothes are ironed, and on your beds."* Mama leaned into the kitchen instructing the three of us to hurry with our breakfast. We were told we would be leaving much earlier than usual Sundays. Moreover, we were moving along at a snail's pace.

"Okay kiddos, lineup, head out, it's time to go." Mama customarily inspected each one of us as we hustled out the door. She made certain we all had our bibles; our hair was brushed and there was no evidence of breakfast on our faces. One of us was certain to receive the fingers that swiftly passed over her tongue to remove a crumb or hold down wild hair. *"Ok. Ok. Ok,"* she would say as each of us passed her inspection and received our pat on the bottom certification. *"Mama, where are we going?"* I asked as we drove a different direction than ever before. *"We are going to Mr. Gary's and Miss Deena's church."*

"Where is it?"

"Just enjoy the drive." Mama said as she began to lead us in a Sunday chorus. We sang until we fell asleep.

"Wake up, babies. We're here." Mr. Gary and Mr. Lamar were waiting to greet us as we entered the huge metal building just off the Gulf Freeway near Scarsdale on the south side of Houston. **Abundant Life Church** was lettered across the front of the building. We entered the sanctuary and were escorted by Mr. Lamar. I turned and looked up to the balcony above one-third of the sanctuary. I could not believe the massive stage or the number of microphones. There was a grand piano, double base drums and a complete orchestra. From stage right, a man dressed in an all-white, tuxedo style suit, climbed the steps and approached the ebony grand piano. The congregation chatter fell silent and all scurried to their appropriate seating. Pastor Jim Johnson began to play the piano like Liberace. The band soon joined as ladies entered the stage and began to sing. People all over the congregation moved to the large isles and danced. This was the coolest church we had ever attended. Our pastor captivated the congregation with stories of flying his airplane but mostly his experiences with signs, wonders and miracles. At the sermon's conclusion seats emptied and lines stretched across the front. People were there expecting a personal miracle of healing in their own lives. It was here that my young eyes witnessed their first REAL miracles.

Mr. Gary, Mr. Lamar and others were positioned in front praying for people with Pastor Jim Johnson. There were men moving behind the people to catch them as they fell back and were laid on the floor. On our way home Mama and Dad inquired if we would like to return next Sunday.

The vote was unanimous. **Abundant Life Church** would become our routine Sunday destination. Mama developed relationships with everyone who assisted in the church functions very fast. We went to lunch with the Pastor's family, Mr. Lamar, and Mr.

Gary's families often. We all enjoyed everything about our new church home. The only downfall was the great distance between our home and its location. Our new church also had a Sunday and Wednesday night service. We began to attend the night service on Sunday as well. Of course, this made Monday mornings difficult for Mama.

CHAPTER 17

"Hey, come on, let's go look at this one." I insisted with extreme excitement as I waved Dee Anne and Michelle to follow me. *"Mama, can we get this one?"*

"No, but follow me." Mama walked us to the back area of the lot. We passed many campers and motor homes along the way. We arrived at a twenty-three-foot motor home that had an over the cab bed just like our camper we went in to **Las Vegas**. The motor home was white with a broad green stripe configuration that contained the words *Free Spirit*. There was a door on both sides of the cab and the front end was just like our appliance store cargo vans. The front grill had the name **DODGE** in its center. Mama gave us the grand tour and demonstrated how the two tables folded into beds and the overhead storage folded down as a bunk bed. It slept eight people. This new motor home would become our Sunday chariot. We now could campout in the parking lot in between services. Mama is an excellent cook and still finds great joy in providing good meals. This new home on wheels provided the privilege of once again enjoying her delicious Sunday lunches. Still, in my opinion, no meal rivals Mama's home cooking with fresh vegetables and hand prepared entrees. Truth be known, I didn't know veggies came in cans until I was a teenager.

I found tremendous acceptance, at our new church and was catching the attention of the entire congregation. There were always three to five beautiful ladies who claimed the microphones at front stage. Not only did they lead the congregation in song, they also performed in a way we had not witnessed prior. Moving forward and becoming the focal point, each one would speak. Their words arrested the hearts of everyone. It was a real time word spoken from the heavens.

Immediately one of the other ladies would step forward and she too would begin to express the heart of God. The most touching was when an individual was pointed out and then heaven's hand wrote a specific note that illuminated their heart.

We became friends with each one of these ladies and their families. Here, in a much greater angelic ambiance, voices harmonized in languages I did not understand. The same experience we witnessed in our living room occurred in most every gathering. People spoke freely of these occurrences and gave biblical reference, explanation and descriptions of many other mysteries. This was what the book Mama read on our **Las Vegas** trip was about.

Summer had passed, and my ninth birthday would fall on a Saturday. I was invited to spend the weekend of my ninth birthday with Mr. Arthur and Deana Guerra. It was this weekend that Mr. Arthur explained that I could experience the things I had been witnessing. After a brief introduction they held my hands and prayed. I do not recall the prayer or the words they asked me to repeat, however I do remember the effect.

The power of the Upper Room described in the book of Acts was now a personal experience of my own. I don't know if there was a tongue of fire dancing above my head, but I do know that there was a fiery enthusiasm bubbling somewhere deep within me. Immediately and without thought or hesitation, I spoke an amazing unknown language. Fully controlled by my utterance, yet unknown to my mind, it ran freely and without thought. It was fluent and annunciated compound syllables. It was not a jibber or repetitive jabbering. It was distinctive, developed and mature in its diction. Evident to Mr. Arthur and Miss Deana was the certainty that a young man of my age could not have created it on his own. Evident to me was the certainty of a new and genuine, fiery experience with Jesus. My excitement was greater than what I came home with from camp. Nothing could ever discount this personal relationship being developed in my life. It was as real as my own existence. Mama was just as excited as I shared what Jesus did in my heart. Mr. Arthur and Miss Deana expressed the same enthusiasm.

I cannot tell you exactly how much time had passed from this weekend to the experience I am about to share. The progression of events became rapid in succession. I had already found my identity in a specific front row seat. My vantage point was directly in front of the grand piano and the ladies with their microphones.

Our family life had become church centric. Everything we did, and everything discussed, revolved around church. Any activities or engagements were scheduled as not to impose on church services or functions. To say we were fixtures at our church was probably an understatement.

CHAPTER 18

Sunday morning service was no different than others. The upbeat dynamic worship time followed by the angelic harmonious slower songs, created its ambiance. This crescendo of aroused emotion was celebrated with the corporate singing in other tongues. Now, because I too had been baptized in fire by Jesus with the evidence of my personal prayer language, I joined in the celebration. My memory of this event is as vivid today as it was 40 years ago. The fiery bubbling deep inside was overwhelming. My hands were raised my arms were stretched and fully extended as if I desired to touch heaven. Although I did not reach heaven, heaven did reach me. The fiery sensation shot from inside me to the palms of my hands. They felt as if they had been wide open in front of Grandpa's blazing fireplace at the **Boots and Saddle Ranch**.

Jeff and I would sit on the ledge of the fireplace after Grandpa had stoked the logs and stacked as many would fit. Our bare backs turned red as we clinched our teeth daring one another to stay and endure the heat. The fire would crack, snap and pop as the heat rose, and the flames climbed. The intensity of the fire was certain to become unbearable and each of us would dart to Grandma, so she could place her open palm on our backs and compare the heat. This event would occur repeatedly with Grandma judging whose back was the hottest.

The heat I felt in the palm of my hands could only be compared to my fireplace experiences. The voices fell silent, but the music continued. Overwhelmed with this fiery feeling, and a butterfly effect in my stomach, tears ran down my cheeks. My hands shook, and my jaw quivered. Something unique, real and outside my explanation was happening in me. I burst out loud enough to be heard by every ear in the massive sanctuary. A dissertation spoken in this new language sounded, without effort or hesitation, from my voice. I do not recall the length of time I spoke, but I do remember there was no pause and Mr. Lamar began to share in English what heaven had spoken through my new tongue. This became a common event as I was urged by the inspirational unction deep within.

Aside from **Abundant Life Church** we attended a multitude of special services all over Houston and surrounding areas. Many of the churches we attended were of like beliefs, but not many were as open to tongues, interpretations and other Holy Ghost experiences.

Soon after this first happened, things began to occur so rapidly that I can't recall their chronological order. However, I do remember many of the key events. It was shortly after I responded to the internal unction that one of the ladies moved forward, called me by name and instructed me with the voice of heaven. *"Troy, you are to begin to give the interpretations yourself, not only of your tongue but those of others as well."*

Once again, during this instruction, I was overwhelmed with the fiery sensation I had experienced before. Only this time, it was not deep within me or in my palms; it was in my vocal chords and my tongue itself. Sure enough, this became the norm. I would respond to the unction and release my angelic language. Then without thought or consideration, I spoke in English. Because of the nature of the things I professed, my acceptance and popularity grew immensely. I was the topic of conversation in multiple congregations.

"That young man is moving in gifts of the Holy Spirit. Did you hear that interpretation?" I would always stand, yet because my stature was still developing it was difficult to see me from most vantage points. However, even when visiting, Mama always made certain we arrived early, and we were positioned near front center. My most memorable experience while visiting another church was in 1978 at **Lakewood Church** in Houston. **Lakewood Church** was about one tenth what it is now. Although it was considered a large church at that time it was small in comparison to its grandeur today. Joel was probably about twelve or thirteen years old. Kenneth and Gloria Copeland were in town and Brother Copeland drew a significant crowd.

The music at **Lakewood Church** has always been amazing. After the last song there was an atmosphere of an undeniable heavenly presence. Were there angels amongst us? I never had a personal encounter but there were many who claimed such presence at these services. The unction came again. It need only be a nudge and my response was certain. I spoke loud and with assertive courage. My voice was clearly heard throughout the three-quarter sphere sanctuary. Several thousand attended here at most services. Once again, I spoke in the well-developed unknown language and immediately backed it with the English interpretation. I had no idea what I was saying in this unknown tongue. I did wonder if this language was spoken by any tribe or nation in the world. I wondered if anyone who heard me understood it. I also had no idea what I would say in English. At ten years old it amazed many and astonished or puzzled others. I merely did what I was urged to do by this fiery gurgling that would rise inside me.

Typically, there was applause of acceptance. From time to time there was an explanation given or words of affirmation from the pastor. This evening I opened my eyes and witnessed Brother Kenneth Copeland move center stage while holding a microphone. I expected he too would give a word that solidified what was just spoken. Instead, I remember these words, *"One day that boy will preach to me."* He then said a few things and gave the que for his back up music. He sang and ministered the most captivating message I ever heard. I recall how I talked with Mama about the ideas he introduced to my heart for days. We became partners with **Kenneth**

Copeland Ministries in 1978. I believe Mama's decision, to partner with **KCM**, has impacted my life in ways I have not recognized. However, the things I do recognize are miraculous.

CHAPTER 19

Mama came out to the alley where I prepared the Bat Mobile to return to the Bat Cave. *"Son, I need you to go in Mr. Aaron's liquor store. I have a few errands to run then I'll be back. Be good for Mr. Aaron."*

"Yes ma'am, I will." I reached out, wrapped my arms around Mama's neck and kissed her just as I still do today. I jumped out of the beautiful blue Eldorado and scurried around the building into the front door of Mr. Aaron's store. Aaron Swearingen is my sister Michelle's God father, but he treated each of us equal in every way. *"Hi, Mr. Aaron,"* I announced as I entered the store. I am sure I enjoyed my typical package of candy corn along with a can of Big Red. My very favorite candy to this day is the same one he introduced me to more than 40 years ago.

When Mama returned to pick me up she announced. *"Someone unlatched my convertible top!"* She was not happy and startled when air penetrated the seal to lift the top. Yes, that was the very important step I had forgotten when preparing the Bat Mobile for its return to the Bat Cave.

I remembered each detail as if it were occurring in real time. So, I shook my head, smiled and chuckled as I looked in the rearview mirror of the Mazda Miata. I inserted the key, turned the ignition and the small 4-cylinder convertible instantly purred. Without hesitation I was backing out the narrow driveway. I parked the car, with its top down, to wait for Carol. The convertible latch sparked a memory in such amazing detail. The human mind is so powerful.

She arrived, and we headed out of town to the countryside. I passed a few places along the way and told her of many childhood experiences. We passed a property Grandpa owned and referred to as the ten-acre lake. I described the paddle barge Grandpa built at the shipyard for Jeff and me. It was about 12 feet long, 5 feet wide and had two large wooden captain's chairs. Each seat had a set of peddles at legs reach. There were sprockets and chains that connected to the large paddle wheel at the rear of the barge. The barge was painted Red, White and Blue. The large letters painted along the side read **THE UNCLE JEFF.** A few miles further lie a four-way intersection we called The Cross Roads. This was a bait shop with live minnow wells in the back. I turned right and sped through the curves as I shifted swiftly through the gears. After about five or six miles, I pulled over in front of the entrance to what once was an amazing dynasty. Only the entry, the perimeter fencing and the large barn remain on the property of amazing childhood memories. The steel letters above the entry read the **Boots and Saddle Ranch**. Carol could see the nine houses, beautiful show horses and childhood memories as I vividly painted them with words. I doubt what we envisioned as we looked across the empty fields was even similar. Although, Carol did show interest in every expressed detail.

I turned the little sports car back in the direction from which we came and at the 4-way turned north. I then suggested we would go to a place where I enjoyed fishing from time to time. We darted up the Farm to Market road and turned off a few miles north of the crossroads. The entrance to the property was less than two miles away. I turned left and eased the low-profile car onto the pasture drive. I began to describe the small lake and how there were a couple of nice oak trees just along the bank. Suddenly the car slowed then almost came to an instant stop. I increased acceleration to no avail. I knew I must act fast. I crossed over a washout that was full of sand.

Aggressively I shifted from first to reverse repeatedly. I would begin to creep then stop. With fearless determination, I could not get the car to come out of the rut.

"Well," I said. *"I'll walk back to the house we passed and see if I can use the phone or maybe someone can pull us out. I'm so sorry."* Carol answered, *"I'll walk with you."* I had turned the engine off and opened my door while volunteering to walk alone. We exited the car, shut our doors and began the walk. I estimate we walked about one hundred feet and then heard a poof. I turned back and saw flames under the center of the car. In an instant I was back at the car and on my stomach frantically throwing sand in an attempt to extinguish the flame. The fire grew out of control. With no hope to put out the fire, I took off at top speed and shouted, *"I'm going for help."* She kept up with me the entire run.

Thankfully there was someone home and they assisted us in calling 911 who immediately dispatched the closest fire department. My second call was to Pastor Frank Lucas. He lived a short distance further up the Farm to Market road. I explained my dilemma and he agreed to drive down to where we were. His son-in-law and the next to youngest of 5 girls were at his home and followed to meet us.

Brother Frank volunteered them to take us back as he quickly expressed, *"You're on your own here son."*

The firemen had completely extinguished any danger. As I approached what remained of the car, my heart sunk. It was burnt to the ground. All four tires were gone, the aluminum wheels melted, the hood was missing and the entire inside was burnt to a crisp. Wow, the first time I damaged any of Mama's cars and I burned it to the ground. It's been twenty-one years and I have yet to drive another car she has owned. I have not even repositioned one in a parking spot.

Our first two dates were spectacular! No one I know could have performed as magnificently as me!

CHAPTER 20

At ten years old I was being recognized by some of the most renowned names in the Full Gospel, Word of Faith, Non- denominational, Charismatic movements. The list would be long. For several years I would speak to children, youth and adult congregations. Of course, the attraction was this boy who was gifted in speaking words of heaven. My relationship with Jesus gave me the confidence to pray for the sick, speak direct and personal words to individuals, boldly proclaim healing and even cast out evil spirits.

I have given much thought to the approach I should take in revealing who I believe was the greatest influence on my 15-year-old life wrecking decision. I have concluded it is of necessity to share what brought my involvement with the church and God to a halt. In consideration of this necessity I must give a brief detail and perspective of what caused this interruption.

Bill Williams was our step-father. He adopted us and participated in raising us for about 14 years. Because of my perspective I chose to limit writings concerning him. I am convinced anti-Christ dogma created his personal internal turmoil defused in our world. Life became crazier and more difficult with increased church activity, Bible crunching and mass tele-evangelist raving. The more he got, the worse he behaved. Yet he relentlessly performed every imaginable activity to get right. How many others have fought so diligently and never found freedom? This is one reason I am encouraged to share my journey.

It was the summer 1980 and Dad planned an event for just me and him. We were going to see a special female guest speaker. I recall others sharing the miraculous occurrences that followed her. Of course, this was why we were going. I remember little about the service, I do remember the speaker was a lady, the facility was small, and we sat on folding metal chairs. After the service she made certain to get our attention. We waited for her to come speak with us. This seemed to be normal in every service we visited where I was nudged by the fiery unction to speak in tongues and interpret.

The tragedy came on the drive home. Bill began to share, again, how *"God had called him"* to be a preacher. The impossible was his ability to interact successfully with people. Mama built relationships and he dismantled them. Anyway, he continued to share how *"God had told him"* that I was no longer to speak in anyway at any church until he was a preacher. Of course, he enforced this message from *"God"* with all the typical text, *"Honor your father...etc."* He explained how God would not bless me, how I would lose my salvation and how he would spank me. Needless to say, my day of the fiery unction's ended. I was around thirteen at the time of this event. It was world changing and re-charted my desired destiny. My identity was removed. There were so many things waring in my young mind I did not understand. Now it seems God rejected me as well. Why would God do this to me? Well, He did not! I always knew when it was the voice of Heaven or the cry of carnality. This was not God, but I was still left with no alternative. I had to seek new acceptance and a new identity.

CHAPTER 21

We drove into Mama's narrow driveway where I backed out her small convertible just a few hours before. I insisted everyone come in as I told Mama about her car. I stepped out of the Suburban and held my left hand back as Carol slid across to grasp my fingers and gracefully join me on the grass. We all four attempted to jockey to the rear, but I was forced to lead. I knocked as I turned the knob and slowly pushed the door open. We all went in. Our presence roused Mama from her Sunday afternoon nap. As I slowly lowered myself to sit on the edge of the couch near her, she inquired, *"What's going on?"* *"Well, Mama, I burned your car to the ground."* She chuckled and said, *"Yeah right."* *"No, Mama, I'm serious, I did."* I don't have the vocabulary to express the look I witnessed on Mama's face, but she never yelled or reprimanded me in anyway. The world has never known a more loving, caring and gracious mother. I can only guess that Mama knows her babies better than we know ourselves. She must know that I am my greatest adversary and impose more condemnation than anyone else could possibly imagine.

Carol invited me to dinner and to follow her home. We became a couple and I began to heap helpings of condemnation on myself in even greater portions than ever before. Although I was happy and accepted I believed I had failed God, failed myself and I had failed my ex-wife. This was the perspective created in my heart from the image of *"God"* imposed on me. Once again, I turned to what I discovered worked. I got high.

I made many world changing decisions in this period of my life. These decisions sent an unborn baby to Heaven, crushed the heart of a sweet Southern Belle and exposed her to things she would have never known if not for my wrong choices. Because of my rapid decline, I ran through her life even faster than my ex-wife's. My inability to accept and forgive myself haunted me. The horrified truth of my life was the more I lived the more I sunk. The more I sunk the more I despised myself.

Thank God for an amazing, loving family who saw me for more than I could envision. Because of their unmerited, never-dying love I made a decision which re-charted my destiny. I agreed to seek help. I called and said *"Mama, I'm ready. Please come get me. I'm at Motel 6 at Westheimer and Sam Houston Toll Road."* Of course, Mama promptly dropped everything and came for me. I said goodbye to Carol and assured her I would get right. My heart quivered in fear that she would not consider another chance. My fear became truth.

Mama took me to wash my clothes and pack. I called the center several times until a voice said, *"Hey, man, just show up and they'll let you in if you really want to be here."* I followed the instructions and went to recovery late 1999.

It was the fall about 2004. The lady telling her story this Sunday night was beautiful. She had silky, long, dark brown hair with long, loose curls. Her skin was olive, perfectly smooth as silk and her amazing brown eyes were round, elegant and twinkled like stars. I listened intently to every word she spoke.

"I was almost eighteen years old. I ran away from home about two weeks before my birthday. It's very difficult for me to explain why or what happened to my life. I was a cheerleader, very popular and in the run for salutatorian of my graduating class. I started drinking my junior year and the occasions became more frequent than the parties I attended. April 1st was not a joke, but it certainly made me feel very foolish. My parents did not allow me to have boyfriends. It was something our church taught about raising a child, so I didn't date. I had too much to drink. He was our high school 'super jock.' It was the first and only time I had sex, and I became pregnant. I knew I was a disgrace and would bring unbearable shame to my family and my church. Not only was I pregnant but my child was inner-racial." She went on to tell when she ran away she met a couple of people on the bus who introduced her to heroin. The stories of losing the power of choice and desiring to quit more than anything imaginable pierced my heart. I knew these failures and willing to bet I knew them even more than she. I never tried heroin but any behavior that controls a life and cannot be shook earns the exact shame.

"They just pulled up to the ER room, opened the door and pushed me out. My water broke just after I bought my last fix. They left me and didn't care if I lived." She explained that she died and described a visit to heaven very similar to the one Mr. Gary Wood told when I was an 8 years old boy. That was twenty-five years earlier, yet I recalled the detail as this young lady described her heavenly encounter. *"I was accepted without question and treated as a Royal Princess. Jesus described my life as flawless, without error and called me His own. I instantly began to breath. I saw Dr. Garcia, Nurse Jackson and his team smiling and patting each other's shoulders."*

Not once did this young lady speak of *"giving an account"* for things past. She did not describe her past flashing before her eyes. She described exactly what the Bible says. The young lady said nothing of her child, nor do I recall much of anything else she shared. She did not speak long but her sincerity and truth were hypnotic. I have never forgotten a detail of her face. I use her as the young girl in the scenario of Chapter 1.

Every attempt, no matter how perfect I performed, did not work. I kept getting high. *"What is the answer?"* I screamed silently from the deepest of remorse and pain. *"Why did God not hear my cry?"* I bashed the gates of hell, petitioned heaven, cried seas of remorse, groveled and crawled in the depths of shame and could not stay sober. More than anything I desired reprieve, healing and freedom from the life destroying vice.

CHAPTER 22

I was about twelve years old, Dee Anne would have been thirteen and Michelle eight or so. We did not know our biological father. We knew very little other than our birth right name. Dee Anne's baby book had a family tree that was partially complete. Mom and Bill were not at home, so we conspired to begin our own private investigation. It wasn't difficult. We have a very unique family name. We learned that our ancestors were the only Ingenhuetts that voyaged to America in the 1890's. Our American ancestry starts at the port of Galveston. They went sixty miles west of San Antonio and became well established in Comfort, Texas. Opa and Oma lived on an original 4,000-acre settlement in Center Point. Comfort's town store, hotel, bank and other mercantile bare our family name.

"Come on Troy, I have it." Dee Anne said carrying her baby book. *"Okay, I'll get the phone book."* I went over to the cabinet where the phone books were kept. It was about 1980 and phone books were a common fixture in every home. The Houston Metropolitan Residential White Pages was as large as the Sears & Roebuck Catalog. It was about 8 1/2" x 12" and every bit of four inches thick.

The Yellow Pages for business advertising was just as large but occupied two books, A-M and N-Z. There was a specific business white pages that made the house hold directory complete. It was only about half the thickness as the other three but listed the businesses by specific name and not category as the Yellow Pages. This comprehensive book collection was a necessity for household phone navigation and had a wide variety of uses. The complete set was a magnificent adjustable booster seat and step stool for growing children. We could depend on a new set delivery every year. It did not require a subscription, reorder notification or purchase. It was guaranteed most every home had two or three years easily assessable. As I grew older and visited more homes, I learned more and more amazing functions of the versatile phone book collection. Every now and again I visit someone who still treasures these obsolete utility tools.

Anyway, I grabbed the enormous Houston Residential telephone book and met Dee Anne at the dining table. We picked up our home phone and placed it between us. The state-of-the-art home phone had a base for the handset which featured a back lit push button dial pad and about a 12' cord attaching it to the wall. Today, the corded, home land line telephone is as much a dinosaur as the phone book itself.

As Dee Anne pointed out the name on the tree she pronounced and read each letter "R-A-N-Z-A-U." I flipped the pages and rattled the alphabet as I got closer to the correct page. *"LMNOPQ, RA, RAN, RAN-Z here it is. Oh, wow, there's only a few of them."* *"I can do it."* I quickly assimilated a script in my head. By the time I dialed the first number I knew what to say. The task became natural by the third call. *"Hi, my name is Troy. Are you Mrs. Ranzau? My sister and I found the last name Ranzau in her baby book's family tree. We're looking for our grandparents and real dad."* *"Yes, I am. Just a moment, let me let you speak to my husband."* Mr. Ranzau informed us that he knew our grandparents and volunteered to hand deliver a message. Ranzau is Oma's maiden name.

"I tell you what. Give me your phone number and I will visit your grandparents. We will be there for ten days. What's the best time to call you when we return?" I said *"Tuesday night, our parents are at an adult Bible study, so we will answer the phone. Thank you so much!"*

I then explained what Mr. Ranzau told me to Dee Anne and Michelle. A mixture of excitement and fear filled our home. We knew this effort would not be accepted by Mom or Bill, but consequence was of no concern. The innate desire to know our father outweighed the inevitable calamity.

I don't know the exact date but there are a few facts of which I am aware. Mom and Bill were married 27 days after they met. I stayed with Grandpa and Grandma on the **Boots and Saddle Ranch** during their honeymoon. This was a monumental event in my toddler's mind. Maybe any young boy would behave the same, or maybe it was an inherent gift that provoked my outburst. This event made an indelible mark, a certain unforgettable impression. Grandma wrapped me in her loving arms with every intention of calming my emotions. I spit in her face, jumped out of her lap, and dove under the dining room table. The iron clad grip; so tender, loving and protecting grabbed my ankle and abruptly halted my escape. Grandpa had a vice-like grip. If he could grasp it there was no escape. His extraordinary strength in his grip brought more fun, love and laughs than anyone could possibly record.

Jeff and I would take turns seeing who could endure the brutal clamping of his hands. We screamed and laughed to the point of tears anytime he was willing to play. That was every time we were willing to take the punishment. *"Just cry Uncle."* Jeff would shout above my scream and Grandpa's laugh. In turn I would laugh, scream, squirm, kick and flop in every attempt to get free. *"Oh yeah!"* Grandpa exclaimed as Jeff bum rushed to free me. One hand gripping my abdomen, pinning me to the carpet, Grandpa grabbed Jeff and in an instant we both were helplessly captive. Screaming, laughing and refusing to cry *Uncle* the grip would only tighten. *"Uncle, calf rope,"* the cry came in unison. Grandma insisted we scat to the kitchen to resuming our Evil Knievel death defying stunts.

Grandpa pulled me out from the dining table as his cowboy belt unleashed across my bottom in one fluid motion. This was my first spanking from Grandpa. I don't recall who cried more. I do remember spending the rest of the night wrapped in his and Grandma's arms.

They both knew my struggle and wept with my confused heart. Grandpa explained why he spanked me and how much he and Grandma loved me. He also told me I was his son, and nothing could ever change his love.

The playful, loving yet painful vice grip hands were tender, caring and safe. This was and will always remain the strength of my heart. Grandpa's hands changed a world and his love is expressed in our hearts forever. I named my son after him and my children know him just as they know GaGa. My son, T.J., was just an infant and Grandpa was 96 1/2 years old when he held him for the first and last time. I said, *"Grandpa he has your name."* Grandpa replied with a tear on his left cheek, *"It's not my name anymore son."* My tears drip on this page as those words resound in my heart. You best believe that is exactly what Grandpa meant as he held his youngest great grandchild. The world is a better place and innumerable lives touched because of Grandpa. We are all world changers, but Grandpa made a significant impact, and many were historical. A book of his life would certainly be worth a fortune. You can give much credit of the writing of this book to **Thomas Jefferson Bryant, Sr**. If not for him and the courage he instilled in my heart you would not be reading it today.

I once said, *"I can't"* to Grandpa and he assured me I could. He said *"The only thing you cannot do is the thing you have not done. The only reason you cannot is because you have not, so just do it."* I have lived by this philosophy and I am certain there is nothing I cannot do. For those of you that know me well know this is one thing I believe.

Mr. Ranzau called us back just as he had promised. He gave us Opa and Oma's phone number. We called and celebrated our findings. We all got to speak to Opa but we did not reunite with the Ingenhuetts until after Opa had passed away. We received letters and birthday cards from them as well as Aunt Diane and Aunt Sharon. I was sixteen or seventeen before we visited **The Ingenhuett Ranch** to reunite with our father's side of the family.

CHAPTER 23

"May I help you?" "Yes, sir" I replied. *"My name is Troy Ingenhuett and I'm parked out front. I've got my bags packed and I need to know if you have a bed open?"* The house manager was extremely agitated and answered abruptly. *"Who told you to just show up?"*

"Sir, I have my bags packed and I need to know if you have a bed." *"I don't know who you think you are but get your smart*&* in here."* *"Yes sir."* I hugged and kissed Mama, then Dee Anne and Michelle goodbye.

I didn't speak much when Mama picked me up from Motel 6. We went to house first. I washed and folded my clothes. I then packed my bag. It was about 36" long, 14" wide and 12" deep. There was an elongated horseshoe shaped compartment on the top between the two handles. Each end of the bag had a large utility pocket with the same style u-shaped zipper top. I had neatly folded every item. The end pockets were filled with toiletries. I had my fingernail and toenail clippers, my typical shampoos, conditioners, body wash, lotion and colognes. I packed for a one-month stay.

We headed to this Deer Park destination. Mama told me that Dee Anne would be joining us. Mama had another pre-determined preliminary stop after we picked up Dee Anne. We pulled into the parking lot of a restaurant and parked. Here was yet another surprise. It was my beautiful baby sister Michelle. There was nothing more heartwarming than to be with the three most beautiful women in my world. Going to a treatment center was a huge breakthrough. This was something I swore would never work and would be a total waste. Although I kept the mass of my addiction hidden for almost seventeen years many knew things were not right. Many of my friends toured a wide variety of these institutions over the previous fifteen years. I had not seen them succeed. As the result my hard-headed philosophies proclaimed how it merely was a matter of having a desire to stop. I boasted how I could put it down anytime if I only had a sufficient reason. However, the significance of a reason sufficient enough seemed to fade time after time.

My first exposure to any sort of drug treatment facility came at about 19 years of age. My best friend in high school was taken to a facility near our home. It was a decision that changed my world forever. He was there for thirty days and we visited on the weekends. There were multiple buildings. The landscape was plush and professionally manicured. The inner courtyard had decorative iron benches that were strategically placed along the winding pea gravel sidewalks. Beautiful decorative cast-iron lamp posts created a picturesque setting. Our visit was short, but we sampled the cafeteria guest menu and toured the building where they held meetings and classes. On-duty doctors and nurses greeted us hospitably. My friend pointed to the male and female dorms. Contemporary up-to-date furnishings and artwork filled the rooms and hallways. This top of the chart drug treatment center was impressive.

However, the monumental world changing impression was the week of his completion. We ventured into a new world for the both of us. Our previous experiences, for the most part, were held to Ecstasy, drinking and marijuana. On Scott Street at a Section 8 project I had the world wrecking introduction of crack cocaine. Within one week we conquered our first intravenous encounter. My life would never be the same.

CHAPTER 24

Two decades later I too was checking into a treatment center. I entered the lower lever of the small two-story structure. There was a metal staircase with concrete steps center of the small building. The balcony stretched across the top floor. The upper level was divided in half. Each side housed bunkbeds and one restroom. As I recall, there was a room crammed with twenty men called the thirty-day house.

The second dorm housed about fourteen who chose to remain longer. It was called the three-quarter house. There wasn't much grass on the lawn area. The tables in the yard were mix matched and there were also warped wooden picnic benches. In spite of its sub- standard features, the yard was kept clean. There was no landscape or cast-iron lamp posts. The sidewalk was cracked with sunken areas that held rain water. Inside the lower level there were a few fold-out tables with metal legs and particleboard tops. The chairs were metal framed with small wooden seats. Men sat at the tables and on the tattered couches. Many greeted me hospitably and inquired if I was hungry. I was not. Mama had fed me at least twice that day.

"Bring your bag over here," a gruff voice announced from the other end of the room. There was a door just beyond a payphone that hung on the wall. The door was open, and I was asked to hand my bag inside and remain at the opening. I could see my bag while it was examined. I assumed it would be searched for drugs or alcohol. There wouldn't be any found in my perfectly packed bag. I watched each item removed, unfolded, examined and then tossed to the side.

Another gentleman then picked it up and waited for the nod indicating yes or no. *Yes,* items went into a thirty-gallon black garbage bag and the no items then went into a bag identical to the first. Item after item received the left to right repeated head shake to indicate management's disapproval. My bag was replaced with a trash bag. I was left with less than 1/3 of the items I packed. I learned things in this journey the average population would not dream possible.

I was relieved of all my toiletries and told I could share deodorant with the other residents. I was told cologne has alcohol and could be consumed. However, most of the other stuff was part of teaching humility along with daily consumption of beans. I had never eaten so many beans in all my life.

A few days later a resident confidentially shared the manager was looking out for my safety. He explained the majority of residents came off the streets and would be jealous of my things. This way of thinking was baffling. How is it possible a person could desire to harm someone because he possesses shampoo, conditioner, body wash, deodorant and a loofa? I couldn't grasp. Of course, no such thing occurred and I met some of the world's finest people. These men differed from those who had written best sellers or greatest hits, won Grammys, Academy Awards, the Nobel Peace Prize and much more only by addiction. We once possessed a magnificent power: the power of choice. We misused this granted love and altered our worlds. Without knowing or understanding when, why, or how, we lost the power of choice concerning using. We had become addicts and alcoholics.

CHAPTER 25

In 1978 the parking lot of **Abundant Life Church** became our routine Sunday hangout. One Sunday near Christmas there was an enthusiasm and excitement that filled the sanctuary greater than usual. It was well into the lunch hour and at least 1/3 of the cars had not left. Center-stage about 8' high was a massive aquarium that held no aquatic life but captivated every eye on a Baptismal Sunday. We were baptized as a complete family! All five of us submerged in unison. I remember the applause and much attention given to us as a family that afternoon.

However, the miracles happening were far more spectacular. People lined up in droves. The Sunday night service was not scheduled to begin for a couple of hours. The parking lot began to fill with cars, and people were anxious to get preferred seating. By this time, I was a front row fixture. Due to the phenomenon of such a young man speaking bold words directly from heaven I was guaranteed my usual seat. I remember the celebration to this day. We witnessed amazing signs and wonders. I stood in line and asked specifically for God to straighten my teeth. You see, that miracle filled Sunday morning my young eyes personally recorded many tangible miracles.

Our friend Gerry Saldana, a lady Mama became friends with, experienced a miracle I witnessed. Gerry had multiple spots on her teeth, touching her gums, of decay. Gerry asked Pastor Jim if she could give a testimony in the Sunday morning service. She stood on the stage with the microphone and told how she had prayed for herself concerning her decayed teeth for several years. *"When I went to the mirror this morning, the black decay was replaced with white fillings."* I remember the shouts of elation, jumping, dancing and shouting that came when she spoke. Sunday night she asked to speak again. *"This afternoon God replaced the white fillings with perfect teeth."* I am certain there were others who know more and remember greater detail of this miraculous event. However, I remember the decay was there before that Sunday morning. Sunday night she went around to everyone who wanted to see her beautiful new teeth. There was NO decay.

We also witnessed a lady's leg grow out. She was forced to buy an entire new shoe wardrobe. A man had been captive to a wheelchair walked normal. Another with a crippled hand found normal function and appearance after decades of dysfunction. Jesus himself must have chosen to visit **Abundant Life Church** that weekend. There were many, many tangible miracles. My teeth remain imperfect today.

Despite my pleading determinations my teeth were not made straight. I remember being so frustrated I refused to leave the church. I proclaimed I would not leave until God straightened my teeth. I was convinced by Pastor

Jim Johnson and Mama that it was okay to go home. I feared God would be upset with me because my faith was insufficient to straighten my teeth. Imagine a fear so strong in a young boy of 10 shook, trembled and cried because he could not please God.

CHAPTER 26

As my bag was being inventoried by the house manager I noticed each man held a book and every book was identical. The hard cover was a common blue. It wasn't royal or navy, nor pool or baby blue. It was just common. I soon learned it was known as **THE BIG BOOK**. The book of Alcoholics Anonymous has formed groups of common peril around the world and saved millions. Its principles and philosophies promise to return the power of choice. The book was written by Bill Wilson and the first 100 people who had recovered in 1935. These people experienced nothing less than a miracle themselves. They believed they found a method that would rid them of all things blocking one from God. As the result, they acquired a conscience contact with the creator of the universe as each one understands Him for themselves. They outlined 12 steps necessary to achieve a successful daily reprieve from alcoholism. Step number nine is the necessity to make right our wrongs. This commitment required approaching those we wronged, admitting how we hurt them and being prepared to make our wrongs right.

Mama picked me up for a lunch date. We ate Mexican food at one of Houston's Metro most famous Mexican food restaurants. The restaurant features authentic enchiladas, fabulous queso, salsa, chips and iced tea. After lunch, I recall leading our conversation to my planned inquisition. I cannot recall our conversation at length, but what I am about to share is something no one could ever forget.

I said something like *"Mama, I know I've hurt you in more ways than I could ever count. I don't know what I could ever do to make it right. But I want to know if you can forgive me?"* The conversation fell painfully silent and her eyes never left the road. I was looking toward her expecting an answer. I anticipated a rapid response. I just knew her answer! It would be nothing less than *"of course, son."* The answer

did not come, and I became extremely uncomfortable. My heart sank. For the first time I feared rejection from my amazing mother.

"Son, I can't do that" was her answer. In an instant, my heart was at the bottom of my stomach. I lost my breath and my entire body seemed to go limp. ***"You're my son, I love you and I have never held anything against you. So, I don't know how to forgive you."***

What I offer you is the very same amazement and reality I experienced that moment. If this is the truth of my mother HOW MUCH MORE is this the heart of our Father God?

Is it possible the Bible is true? Is it possible that Jesus accomplished that which he came to do? Are the wrongs of the world forgotten and put as far as the EAST is from the WEST? Is it possible that we are Holy, Blameless and above reproach? **Yes, it is**!! God's answer is different. I assure you as a child of God His answer to a request of forgiveness is *"I don't know what you are referring to. I have NO recollection!!"*

My truth is this. I have done even more and created greater pains for my family since this day with Mama. Yet to this day, they are not counted against me. I have not lost my status, my position or love with my family. They have not cast me out or separated from me. If they have not, and certainly had shortcomings of their own, why would God? If one is to believe He will or that He does, then they believe Jesus failed and God is a liar. As for me, I must believe Jesus.

He has shown me His heart through Mama more than just this one time, and He has shown His never-ending commitment no matter what I do, over and over again.

There is no other explanation to the life I live. It's not that it seems this way, it is without refute an evident fact. I live a life of unmerited favor. The idea of a young boy who spoke mind riveting heavenly words was but a beginning. It's never stopped. God's favor never quit. From my perspective, it's as if the more I persisted in self-reliance the more evident His unmerited favor became. No matter how bad I behave God will not let go.

This is the antithesis of most religious thinking. My life is the epitome of Grace!! No matter what I destroy just around the corner is an opportunity with greater promise. In relation to what should have been obtained, I am a disappointed mishap. However, I am a miraculous life of great hope. Despite my bullheaded rejection of God my sail is now set to a destiny of fulfillment with Him.

The three months and twenty-four days stay in the treatment center was not the answer. I learned more about how to consume cocaine, where to acquire it and pay less than I learned about staying sober. I met men who suffered the same loss of choice and sought companionship while getting high. It was not long, and my condition seemed to be more highly advanced than before I sought help. My only hope was the short period of sobriety accomplished. Although it seemed small, life for a day without the thought of using was nothing less than miraculous. I dreamed big dreams of success and accomplishment to prove my worthiness. I imagined the legacy I would create to overcome the shame I had forged. Proclamations and resolutions of how I would never again travel the roads of loss and degradation continued. I meant every word. I was certain of my fortitude, ability and commitment. Yet I once again hung my head in great shame. I could not muster the power to choose. How and why remains a mystery. Even to this day, I cannot explain with sufficient evidence how or why I went back. But I did.

I was still at the treatment center Christmas of 1999. As I think about Christmas growing up I remember smiles and laughter. There are spectacular life moments surrounding this cheerful time of the year. Every Christmas was a guaranteed fabulous festivity filled day at the **Boots and Saddle Ranch** and at GaGa's too. As you must also have Christmas traditional favorites so do I. Grandma's chicken & dumplings, GaGa's Yum Yum salad, bon-bons and the hand rolled spinach balls are top of the chart. Nothing beats the left-over turkey sandwiches made with Miracle Whip and cranberry jelly. Like most all gatherings the men watched sports, the ladies were in the kitchen and the kids ran and played. Although at GaGa's I could be found in the kitchen. Even now I prefer the preparing of the feast, love and conversation in the kitchen over sports any day.

Our Christmas trees, like most American middle-class families, were bulging of presents. Gifts ranged from beautiful new outfits, everyday clothes, shoes, necessities, toys, bikes, games and the *"oh wow"* present that thrilled us all! There was the present I wanted and asked for the previous three to nine months. Santa Claus never missed our house until we learned he is pagan. By the way my children believe in Santa Clause and I will insist he is real for as long as they are willing to believe.

Santa Claus was removed like many other memorable traditions and events of past time family fun. Halloween became forbidden, Easter no longer had a bunny and egg hunts ended. Many childhood joys were tainted with unacceptance by God. Celebrating such things somehow altered God's love and qualification of His bounty.

This way of believing rapidly flooded every dimension of our lives. Holidays became about church events. Extra-curricular activities were eliminated when predicted to interfere with church functions.

Community functions were labeled forbidden, of the Devil and demonic. There was no longer traditional music heard in our home and television was held hostage by Bill. Every precaution advised was adopted in full measure. We were not permitted to violate these new God statutes or offend the dogmatic opinions of preachers. This idea of being tainted and not accepted by God aroused fear and much strife in our home. Outsiders were ostracized as if plagued with a leprosy called heathen, sinners and worldly. People were ridiculed according to their chosen denomination and viewed as less approved by God. Fighting for God's approval was exhausting. The required performances made us seem weird to our friends. Multitudes flocked to Jesus, yet we were avoided. How could what we were doing be the life of acceptance and promised favor? Dream careers became of ill repute and this thing we were commanded to become was tumultuous.

I was almost 15 years old and Bill gladly took a voluntary layoff from Gulf Oil. He was a computer hardware repair man. Chevron purchased, and Gulf offered a small package. This was his opportunity and last-ditch effort to rid his life of his self-centered agony. He believed he was *"called"* to be a preacher, and **Rhema Bible College** was the solution to becoming suitable for God. His answered prayer was our opportunity to be free of his strife filled personality. Love and harmony immediately filled our home. Stress and confusion left with him. Our family was in a financial low but there was peace and joy we had only dreamed.

Mama, Dee Anne, Michelle, and I knew there was no money for the elaborate Christmas gifts of our past. We didn't have the money to purchase a Christmas tree. Christmas Eve of 1983 the local Kroger grocery store was giving away the trees they did not sell. Together we tied red ribbon bows, white ribbon bows and red bows with white polka dots. We only had one strand of tiny twinkle lights for our little tree, but our hearts sparkled with a true Christmas joy we had not known! There were no presents exchanged, but the love, peace and joy that filled our home from each of our hearts made this the best Christmas ever.

CHAPTER 27

I completed the thirty-day regiment of the **Wheel House** in Deer Park, Texas. My accomplishment awarded me the privilege of having my car and employment. The first day searching for employment I received a management position down the street from the treatment center.

Christmas Day came and two of the men joined me for Christmas at Mamas. I was greeted by Mama with the most beautiful love filled smile and open arms you can envision. There was acceptance, love in her embrace and a special sense of pride. I reintroduced the men as we entered her home. Suddenly, I stopped. I have no words to express the rush of emotions and the joy that overtook me. In the small parlor room were Mama's baby grand piano and the Christmas tree. My vantage point adamantly insists there were rays of glory coming from heaven. There stood the simple tree with one strand of lights, red ribbon bows, white ribbon bows and red ones with white polka dots. Even now I can see the joy filled tears on Mama's face as she presented this gift. The sad truth is not even the peace, joy and love of this acceptance held the effect necessary for me to remain sober. This was Christmas of 1999; fifteen years had passed but the love of the best Christmas ever was never forgotten.

Three months later I migrated back near family and re-engaged in Mama's home church. Things once again began to spiral out of control. It seemed the more effort I gave to perform appropriately, the more difficult it was to maintain sobriety. In fact, near impossible. Once again, I was overcome with the shame of relapse. Three years after the second coming of the Christmas tree around Mother's Day, I made another life changing decision. I heard of a special haven where discipleship, bible teaching and AA are used to create sobriety. I announced to my beautiful sisters I was giving the only Mother's Day gift I could muster. I was checking in the very next morning. This time was different. There was no intervention or outside influence. I made a logical conclusion and located a facility that boasted the combination effort of AA and Jesus. The last four years of excruciating efforts to produce an everlasting effect of sobriety convinced me neither the methods of the church or AA alone was sufficient for me.

There was a camaraderie and excitement in the fellowship of men looking for a common solution. Although what we had chosen was a wide variety of different elution producing cocktails, the end results were very similar. Chaos, confusion and heartache reigned and triumphed in the lives of us all. Once separated from our debacles everyone had amazing promise. The hearts and spirits of our families connected in hope and relief. All from many different walks of life, meeting with similar ambitions and connected in the most unexpected ways. I revisited a night of consumption and in accordance to the program's handbook I was required to leave for a 30-day period. I returned in about six weeks and stayed much longer this term.

It was different, as I mentioned there was something happening I could not pinpoint or even describe. As in every setting I've been, I gained great favor and was appointed responsibilities above my constituents. But this obviously is not what I am referring to.

Somewhere in the unsettled subconscious of frustration, I began to embark on ideas of truth in total contradiction of what I was raised to believe. Fifteen years I refused the concept of being any part of things labeled or proclaiming to be about God. Yet, God was revealing His love and truth to my heart.

One day I was working on a construction project to house more men. I had many life changing encounters when working with Bob, but this one marks an astonishing turn to understanding forgiveness. Bob Mersmann, founder of **The Manna House** in Brookshire, Texas, asked me, *"Troy, what is it that keeps causing you to go back out?"* I answered something like this…… *"I don't know Bob I just don't like Troy. I can't forgive him for things he did to hurt his family and especially his wife and then his girlfriend Carol."*

Bob continued by asking me, *"Do you believe God has forgiven you?"* "Of course, I do", I proclaimed. *"Over 2000 years ago on the cross, He forgave me of everything past, present and future. He took away the sins of the world and that didn't leave me out!"* Emphatically, I proclaimed the truth. I believe these words rang deeper in my heart than in his. But it was his next words that cut me deep. *"Then what makes you so much better than God that you can't forgive yourself?"* Needless to say, I had no answer to that question. In fact, I still review the question as I find myself in regret for things I do wrong. Although I find it natural and almost effortless to not hold a grudge towards others I regularly battle a self-repugnance for the heartaches I created for those I love.

The shame of this common affliction is its source. Pulpits that preach sin consciousness destroy hearts. These traditions have been handed down for centuries and continue to destroy God's purpose. Jesus made us right. He paid more than double the necessary price of any needless self-repugnance. Ideas that impose a necessity of pleading for acceptance are anti-Christ. These impositions are in opposition of the cross. They literally shout Jesus failed! He did NOT FAIL!! He not only accomplished the requirement to relieve our debt, He over did it by more than double. Jesus took our account. He took the account for the entire world past, present and future. If I believe that God keeps track of my wrongs and expects me to grovel in remorse, then I believe He is a liar and made a spectacle of Jesus in vain. I can NOT believe this is of God. I can NOT believe He is bipolar, schizophrenic and believe He is my provider. These concepts do NOT work. My opinion is that many people struggle to experience life as God intends because dogmatic anti-Christ doctrine plagues the Church.

The most accomplished work of the Devil must be the devaluing of Jesus' accomplishments and of our intrinsic worth.

Unfortunately, my insight of God's belief in me is minute in comparison to His truth. My greatest persuasion is my life itself.

CHAPTER 28

One afternoon, about lunchtime, I had a visitor come to my office. She led the praise and worship team, taught Adult Sunday school classes, and invoked many to be *"spiritual."* She was admired for her devotion to the ministry. Everyone who knew me had knowledge of my struggle staying sober. It was evident whenever I slacked in participation of church events and services. I no longer sat on the front row or joined in the frothy emotional crescendos of celebration. Under other circumstances I would have been excited about her arrival, however it was evident in her demeanor she did not come to encourage me. She asked to speak to me privately. I do not recall the entire conversation but the words I do recall were these.

"Troy, God told me to come here and tell you that this is your last chance. If you don't get right with Him, He is going to wash His hands of you."

Thank God she used His name in vain. God would never make such a proclamation. Saying God-plus an exclamatory is NOT using His name in vain. Using His name to validate ideas contrary to Jesus is using the Lord's name in vain. Isn't it amazing how many ideas do just that?

This vile opinion haunts the minds and hearts of so many people I have met. Our value is focused on how we look, how we dress, the way we talk, with whom we socialize, what denomination we choose and even how we choose to wear our hair. If we get God's perspective, how much he loves and cares for each of us, we would never question our acceptance. There would never enter our thinking or never be a question of being in His will or if we please Him. The truth of creation is this; **WE ARE HIS WILL AND HIS PLEASURE!!**

CHAPTER 29

I cannot tell you exactly what happened, but this God confrontation was much more aggressive than the one at age 15. I was exhausted, fed up and furious. My life consisted of one disappointment and then greater ones stacked on even greater ones. Parades of hurt greeted the let down and disgusted people that now distanced themselves from me. There was probably not a single accomplishment that wasn't followed by a greater debacle. I lived an astonishing bottle rocket life. Time after time I launched from the dirt and shot to the top only to pop and fall to pieces.

"What happened?" "Why did you?" "I don't understand." "How could you?" These were the questions of many. I wanted it to end. I was a focal point of judgement and bewilderment. I wanted the answer, the solution, the cure. More than my next breath, I wanted to live accepted, loved and accomplished. I did not care why I did the things I did. It was all my making and the grip became much stronger and more powerful than me. I was looking to rid my existence of guilt and shame. My self-imposed condemnation held me captive to a life of failure and addiction.

The pages would be endless if I wrote of the five years that sculpted my personal devaluation. The hot pursuit of *"God"* and all the mysterious signs and wonders devastated my self-perception.

However, the fact remains steadfast and true that I had an intimate and personal contact with Jesus. He not only touched me, He enveloped me, sealed me and called me His own. No matter where I went, what I did or how pitiful I behaved He NEVER left me, NEVER forsook me and NEVER gave up.

I stood at the jumping off point. Just like the morning I lay on the living room floor of the vacant apartment in Dallas, but I now ranted to God. This time, so no one would hear me, I drove out to the countryside down a long dirt road. I parked on the roadside, got out of my car and yelled. *"You know what God, this is ALL BULL *0#&!!!"*

I did not hold my tongue or with strain my vocabulary. My anger was directed to God personally and I wailed more explanatories to Him than I've heard any person spew towards anyone. My intent was to insure God understood exactly how I felt about it all.

"Look" I said, *"it comes down to this."* My tone became rational and I was ready to come to terms and end this explosive confrontation. *"I either have to believe EVERYTHING I have been told about You is wrong, or I have to believe that You do not exist. I cannot believe You are not real, but I can't believe what I have been taught either."*

This decision proved to be the most dynamic decision I had made up to this point. The tide changed. I discarded all the junk that opposed Jesus and determined to reject any concept that put the focus on me. I had successfully proven to the world and to myself that I could not. If left to me I am doomed. The funniest part of my conclusion is it was exactly what God wanted. I confronted God and He embraced me. I cussed Him every direction and He blessed me more. Please do not get the idea I am declaring to cuss God out to obtain blessing. On the contrary, I was seeking Him in spirit and truth. I was aroused to the highest of emotions. I shouted to the top of my lungs, shook my fist in the air and kicked dust from the ground. I created a real pep rally that others would have joined my cause with shouts of *"THAT'S THE SPIRIT"* if any had been near. I held nothing back and spoke exactly what became my perception of truth. I did so directly to God and He responded with **Amazing Real Hope**.

Today I laugh as I remember the fit I threw. I am certain God got quite a chuckle from my performance. I left this God confrontation with a since of peace, comfort and hope I had never known. In addition to His obvious embrace there now rose from deep inside me a kicking compulsion to search, dig and to find truth.

CHAPTER 30

I am very fortunate to have met so many wonderful people. There are some that seem to have an element of perfection in timing and influence. I believe this is true with Mr. Al Finch. Al is one of the most focused and unique personal mentors I have met. It would take at least a chapter to include his accomplishments in one on one ministry. He has over 40 years of mentoring men and assembling inner-active lessons that encourage an intimate relationship with Jesus. Not only did Al introduce me to a mass of books and authors but he also showed me how to find my identity in Christ. Al started our meetings with specific instruction. *"I want you to read the book of John. Every time you see the word believe, believes, believing, or any form of the word, circle it and understand its instruction."*

I completed Mr. Finch's assignment in a few sittings. I counted one hundred and marked them with a circle in the twenty-one chapters of John. This simple assignment solidified the one and only requirement to receive God's eternal life. Believe in Jesus!

No matter how dogmatic or charismatic any position shouts, it cannot shake my footing as the result of this simple assignment. I had read the New Testament a few times. I had read the account of John but now there was something real, something new. It was as if God turned on a new part of my mind. There was an astonishing new understanding alive inside me. It raced from one dot to the next drawing a picture of perfect clarity. I didn't fast or pray or take some special sabbatical. I did nothing fancy, spiritual or heavenly. Fact is I did just the opposite. I cussed God out and proclaimed all that hyper- spiritual, hocus-pocus, mystical humbug stuff was bunk. The crazy confusion of previous ideas crumbled away and lost their grip on my mind.

The corridors, hallways and parking lots of churches across our nation fill with idle chatter of the state of our nation and the wrongs of those not there to defend themselves. Judgement, accusation and rejection of God's children are heartbreaking. *"We really need to keep so and so in our prayers…"* is used to justify ridicule and slaughter those whom God holds and cherishes. This is what seems to be groomed and cultivated by *"Christian"* dogma.

God SO loved the <u>WORLD</u>! Jesus took the world back and put it into the hands of its rightful ownership, you and me. But doctrines and traditions have caused us to curse and call the creation above the angels vile and distasteful. We are God's favored and chosen home. My determination to know Jesus and His purpose became stronger and stronger. The more contradictions I uncovered, the more I searched. I later learned how effectively this transfigured many lives. A dear friend of mine has a church today in which he accredits its birth to these and other challenges. His beautiful, pristine wife told me how she could not understand my position.

"I said to Phil, 'Why can't he just go with the flow.' I just thought you were being arrogant." Johnna smiled and laughed thanking me for stirring the pot.

Many found my statements harsh and even difficult to wrap their thinking around. I did too but it was part of this journey to Grace and Truth. My heart anticipates you will know Jesus in a way you never dreamed, through my personal accounts of His Amazing Grace. I believe you will know Him, from this time forward, like never before.

CHAPTER 31

Unfortunately, without thought of my previous disgrace and disappointments, I found myself high. I already knew this would end my stay at **The Manna House**.

Amazing Grace! I once again was climbing the opportunity that naturally came my way. But the grips of addiction drug me to plunder, and this time I would return to **The Manna House** without the privilege of choice. There were restrictions placed on me that would prevent me from gainful employment. I was bound to the property of **The Manna House** unless accompanied by staff, family or an approved escort. I returned to raising funds and gaining donations for the ministry. I worked full time on expansion and improvement of the property. We doubled the chapel size and added another bunk house with a laundry room. We built a tool shed and about an acre of donated pavestone was laid out as walks and patios. I don't recall all that was donated as I informed the community of who we are, where we are and what we do; but there was an astonishing amount. The awareness encouraged a multitude of businesses and individuals to participate in the purpose to free addicts.

I once again enjoyed working with Mr. Bob Mersmann. We didn't always agree and in several of our conversations we vehemently disagreed.

"Troy, we will always be sinners. We will sin every day. Jesus is the only perfect one. We have to strive to be more like Him, do the best we can and ask for His forgiveness when we fail."

"If that's true Bob, then why did Jesus tell everyone to 'sin no more? Why did Peter and Timothy tell us the same and John tells us that we can't even sin?"

"So, are you saying you will never sin, Troy?"

"No, no, no. I'm just saying there must be an answer. If the answer is the cop out we've been taught, then God is a liar and Jesus failed. It has to be better than that."

Our conversations were often challenging and always encouraging. Bob never discouraged any concepts or opinions. Instead he always gave grace and direction. Bob typically answered my contentions by suggesting we both study to find the answers.

"Sir, you know I'm not saying I'm right? I'm just saying there are way too many holes in many theologies. Just because I disagree doesn't mean I'm right. But it doesn't mean I'm wrong either." Soon we found a common smile and laughter with the condensed statement. ***"Doesn't mean I'm RIGHT; doesn't mean I'm WRONG either!"*** This statement would dissolve any misunderstandings from wrangling. I still live by this understanding today. I may find exception when I hear the Word presented. However, this does not mean it's wrong. Nor does it mean it is right either. It just means I take exception. These

exceptions rekindle words spoken by Pastor Lucas. *Find out for yourself!*

CHAPTER 32

In 1974 I was in the first grade and Mama enrolled me in T-ball. *"Keep your eyes on the ball. When you complete your swing, the bat should lay across your shoulder and flat against your back. Your head never moves. You will always keep your head still with your eyes right here on the ball! Watch closely as I swing again."* This was the simple, clear-cut directions given by my T-ball coach. I had absolutely NO problem understanding and following these "How to's."

Coach Frankie instructed us on the fundamentals of how to grip, hold and swing the bat, how to step into the swing, how to follow through and even how to stand and direct the ball wherever we willed. These specific step-by-step how-to directions were so precise in every intricate detail I visualized my perfect swing long before I ever even held the bat. He continued to go over and over each detail and every facet while demonstrating frame by frame instructions.

Although this demonstration was viewed about forty-three years ago, I too can still teach the correct how-to fundamentals of swinging a baseball bat. We watched, listened and imagined ourselves smashing the white ball stitched with red twine distances that The Babe himself would envy.

After rounding the bases for the record-breaking homerun every fan in America chanted my name as the Astrodome's foundation shook from foot stomping, jumping and applause. Confetti and streamers filled the Eighth Wonder of the World celebrating my certain Baseball Hall of Fame position. Just as I crossed home plate my coach jolted me with a sharp alert: *"Pay attention Troy, you're next."*

Each one of us was given the opportunity to practice every detail of the precise fundamental instructions we received. I blushed as I realized my coach had caught me deep in my own imagination. He placed the bat in my hands, stood behind me and again went through every aspect of properly addressing the baseball swing. His arms draped around my shoulders. He perfectly positioned my hands, feet, hips, shoulders, head, eyes and body. After insuring every perspective was in unison to fundamental perfection, he then guided my entire physic through the proper fluid motion. I was soon ready to launch out on my own. Because of these accurate detailed instructions and coaching techniques, we finished the season in first place. He presented the same detail to fielding, throwing and running as batting. At the season's conclusion, I was presented with a 1st place trophy identical to the ones every member of my team received. In addition to our first-place trophy, I was presented a separate trophy recognizing me as the Most Valuable Player of the league that season. There was an almost certainty of a home-run hit at every bat. I had acquired the skill necessary to place the ball where ever my coach directed.

To this day friends of Mama reminisce about the captivating feats in the games they remember I played. There were those who came out just to see what excitement would be aroused as the result of the short, blonde-headed wonder. Mama talks of having to alter jeans by cutting and hemming them at the knees when found to fit in the waist. Grandpa shared stories of how my short legs made me clumsy.

"You're the only person in the world who falls upstairs, son." I can still see his laughter as he would talk of opening the car door and saying, *"Fall out Troy."* However, these short, stout gifts from God ranked me as one of the fastest and certainly the quickest amongst all competition. The most talked about baseball memory was the run I scored twice in one game by *hot boxing* my way through each base into home. Parents of both teams applauded and cheered me even greater than the imaginary crowd of my Astrodome heroic day dream. Unfortunately, my baseball celebrations were ended after our move to join **Abundant Life Church**. This childhood extra-curricular activity was certain to interfere with the church life mandates.

CHAPTER 33

It was my last time at **The Manna House** sometime in 2003 and I spent as much time with Al as he permitted. *"What is Faith?"* Al Finch inquired. *"The substance of things hoped for and the evidence of things not seen."*

"How did you know that?" *"Hebrews 11:1."* I responded with absolute certainty.

"That's close but that's not exactly what Hebrews 11:1 says." Mr. Finch challenged.

"What do you mean? Of course, it is." My head shook curtly as I rapidly thumbed the pages to locate the eleventh chapter of Hebrews. *"Right here…it says…Now faith is the…"*

"What?" Al quickly cut me off with a smile and a chuckle while lowering his reading glasses and peering across the table.

"Now faith is the substance of things hoped for the evidence of things not seen." I read. *"NOW faith is."* Al repeated annunciating the word **NOW**.

"So, what is hope?" He inquired. *"Uh, uh, uh…"* My mind raced as I attempted to assimilate the proper definition without using the word Hope to define it. *"….uh, expecting good stuff."* Once again Al pulled his reading glasses down and chuckled while peering across at me. *"Did we already do this exercise?"* He asked. *"No sir, what do you mean?"* *"Did someone else share it with you?"* *"No!"* I demanded and shook my head. *"Why, what's wrong?"*

"What's the difference between faith and hope?" I could see Mr. Finch was positive he had stumped me. I wasn't quite sure how to answer, nor was I sure I knew the answer. My mind quickly deduced logically so I responded. *"Faith is certain, Hope is expectant."*

"Write this down." Al had given very specific instructions of what he expected prior to our meeting. Our first meeting was an introduction with the Book of John assignment. He then gave a list of things I would need for this second meeting. So as instructed I had my specific notebook where I would be writing as he dictated. He explained in precise detail how to header the page then to write Hebrews 11:1 exactly as it read.

"Below that write Hope: The confident expectancy that something good is going to happen. Skip a line, then write Faith is now, Hope is in the future." *"So"* Al said, and paused as he once again peered across at me with a look of challenge. Along with this new question came the exact same chuckle as he inquired. *"How do you get faith?"* *"By hearing the Word of God"* I said instantly.

I still laugh as I recall Al's belly felt chuckle. He flipped his pages to see the backs that faced me then looked around as to see if I may have found a reflecting object somewhere behind him.

"Okay, I don't remember where that one is, but it says, Faith comes by hearing and hearing the Word of God."

"So, do you get faith by reading the Word of God.?" Al inquired. *"Well, sure."* I answered. *"No!"* he demanded. This time he laughed and removed his glasses. I read his body language perfectly. Al was very proud he stumped me. *"Faith comes by hearing, not by reading."* Chuckling uncontrollably for an instant Al then said, *"So you have read out loud."* *"So where did you learn about faith?"* He asked. *"Well, I don't know."* I said reluctantly. *"You know who Kenneth Copeland is, right?"* *"Well, of course."* Al answered.

"I guess I learned most everything about faith from him. That was more than twenty years ago though. So, I don't remember much." Al chucked again and said *"Most all of my lessons are from his teachings."*

I wasn't that surprised but since Brother Copeland was one of my very favorite childhood Bible teachers we struck common ground. *"My best friend, through junior high, his Dad is Kenneth's cousin."* Al insisted I buy a copy of the book, ***The Holiest of All*** by Andrew Murray. I was instructed to read a chapter a day, but I couldn't set the book down. This reading began the absolute solidification of The Once for All Sacrifice, Jesus Christ. Al also directed me to read a regiment of daily affirmations. His instructions were to read them *out loud* three times a day. He further instructed: *"Every time you see 'in Him,' 'in whom,' 'in Christ,' 'in the Beloved,' 'in Christ's,' BELIEVE IT!*

This is OUR identity, this is who we ARE!! I want you to affirm these, so they become your first thought."

I don't recall how far along, how many lessons or books I had completed but I was situated to study and read more than most other residents. I vowed to make the best of my time. GaGa instilled in us a philosophy of gratefulness. *"If you can't smile about it Foy Foy, then it's not worth thinking about. We will always have something to be happy about because we have each other. We have family."* This is one of my favorite things GaGa gave us. These were not words that shifted with the winds or subsided with the tides. This was her heartbeat; her breath and the evidence of GaGa's love. This faithful truth is still lived today in each of our homes.

CHAPTER 34

I remember the summer of 1979. Billy Williams, Bill's eldest son, visited us again. There were many times he came to visit and even some he briefly lived with us. Those occasions typically ended abruptly with an angry confrontation between Billy and Bill. As I mentioned, this was common concerning any relationship Dad had with anyone.

As the result of our new *Crazimaniac* emendation, many were persuaded that ALL life's unacceptable issues were due to the devil and or his minions. Countless stories of demonic exorcisms filled services, gatherings and even luncheons. We heard their names, their duties, their relationships, positions and their terror. Whenever there was an event on the news or whenever someone's personality was deemed unacceptable, the devil and his roustabouts received the glorified responsibility.

Several men from **Abundant Life Church** gathered in the living room of our two-story home. Center of the room were the wooden chairs brought from our dining table. One for Billy was dead center of the circle formed with the others. Dee Anne, Michelle, and I were instructed to stay upstairs. We were not permitted to be downstairs that evening. However, the loud and obnoxious ranting plus the banging commotion insured I'd sneak a peek. Tip toeing downstairs I witnessed the live and true account of the exorcist. The physical contortions and expressions of Billy were not as theatric as all the screaming, demanding and whaling in tongues heard from the spiritual hierarchy. In fear of being spotted, I hustled back upstairs to report my observations.

As indelible this event may seem, it was the crusade aftermath I remember most. Concluding the at-a-boys, explanations, sharing of previous encounters and so on, everyone left our house. This is what I remember most. Bill with a bottle of olive oil in hand walked to every corner in our home. Whether it was EVOO or just your basic olive oil, I don't recall, but Bill splattered every cabinet, closet, attic hatch, under the beds and tables. He drizzled the oil while ranting the same gibberish I overheard earlier. He was shouting into these spaces as if the demons had sought refuge in the nooks and crannies of our home.

I watched in bewilderment then inquired why this unnecessary performance was going on. *"What are you doing?"* I asked. *"You don't want the demons to get you, do you?"*

"They can't get me! They're scared of me. They were scared when they saw me at the bottom of the stairs." This absolute truth earned me the commonly received punishment of a belt spanking for disrespect.

Pieces of apron and handkerchief used to wipe Paul's sweat were sent across the land. Those who received theses garment remnants experienced healing and evil spirits (demons) fled. If this is true for Paul, then trust my words the devil is scared of my dirty socks!!

What I witnessed at twelve years old remains an absolute. The instant Billy made eye contact with me, over the shoulders of the screaming men, the demons left him. I never winced or blinked. I was not frightened, concerned or alarmed. My step-brother, whom I loved, was in torturous pain. I whispered in silence as to not be heard by Bill, in fear of the ramifications for my disobedience. *"Stop it now!"* Billy's expression of release was immediately followed by new turmoil. *"Quit!"* Both whispered demands caused hell to tremble. The demons without resistance left Billy. I do not believe there is any other necessary ceremonial craziness required when a person desires freedom. I also know the task was complete. I can't explain how but I just KNEW. The same way I knew I was to follow the messages in tongues with the English explanations I also KNEW Billy was free.

CHAPTER 35

My responsibilities at **The Manna House** kept me on the property more than not in 2003. Routine has never intrigued me. I prefer to live spontaneously. This too has its pros and cons. As a result, I cannot tell you exactly what I was doing but it definitely wasn't as interesting as what I witnessed.

One of the co-founders was walking the property. I watched closely as he moved from tree to tree. He stopped at each tree for a moment then continued to the next. This captured my attention because he was carrying the familiar olive oil bottle. I noted as he tilted the bottle to soak his finger and dabbed the oil on the trees. The act itself wasn't strange. He was anointing or smearing on olive oil. It is biblical in reference and holds powerful validity. Therefore, I was curious in finding out the details of his endeavor.

Later I was in the office with Pastor Dan and my friend Ron Albright. I respectfully inquired about what I had witnessed. He explained how he was creating a *hedge of protection* from demonic forces. This detailed explanation including other personal reflections and was supported by Ron's verbal authentication. I listened intently but my mind raced back to my personal experience and without thought or hesitation I responded.

"You're kidding me, right? Well, you don't have any concern as long as I'm around, sir! They're scared of me. The same Spirit that raised Christ Jesus from the dead lives in me!"

I too shared opinions and experiences to support my declaration. This included my witness of the account with Billy. In addition, I explained two exorcisms where I had hands on involvement. I also shared an account in Deer Park at **The Wheel House** where I first sought recovery in 1999.

A man who lived in the woods with the homeless showed up for help. He was treated with the same hospitality given to every resident. He displayed a distinguishable evidence of *crazy*. The next morning the house manager said he found the man on the steps in front of the building. He was on the landing ranting some crazy gibberish totally nude. Of course, this accelerated all the conversations concerning him. I was drawn to talk to him. I introduced myself, but he never looked my direction. I wish I could remember my curious inquisition but what I do remember was touching him on the forearm.

"Why did you burn me?" the man shouted as he recoiled and intently looked away. Curiously I touched him with my finger tips on his shoulder. He jumped up and screamed *"Please stop burning me!!!"* This time he momentarily made eye contact. Physically trembling he said, *"They don't like it."*

"Do you want them to leave?" I asked. This question came without thought. His countenance changed, and he looked away.

"NO", a guttural voice answered that was distinguishably different than his. The man walked out the door, down the front sidewalk and disappeared. I never saw him again.

There were no such examples given by Pastor Dan or Ron but there was the *"They say"* and *"So and so said"* reports expected to sway my opinion as it had theirs. It did not. My truth is from personal experience. I don't doubt some have had experiences they described but I have not.

Ron's input was unforgettable. *"Be careful!"* he warned.

"Why? What do you mean?" I asked.

"I'm just saying..." as if to imply such bold declaration would expose me to an impeding danger. I absolutely understood why Ron had this opinion.

Ron and I had met in our pre-teen years. Our families toured and attended the same church circles. He had learned the same ideas as I had growing up. It is true that many others have the same concepts.

I left the office with thoughts of confirmation along with doubt and a tinge of confusion. I also shared that I did not believe demons could just hang out on earth and especially not around me. My understanding convinced me they must have residency with a living soul.

"God, show me what I said is true. If it's not, prove it to me." These are the words I whispered as I walked across the property to my car. Ideas of the devil putting thoughts in my mind, attacking me, oppressing, influencing and even listening to intercept my prayers never seemed to appeal to me as a child. I had discarded most all of them after my first confrontation through Billy. I reasoned that if Jesus successfully defeated the devil then these concepts were invalid and of no concern to me. I find no reference to omnipotent existence other than God Himself. I am certain, beyond refute, that the devil never was and will never be all powerful, all knowing, or in more than one place at one time. Therefore, not being God or possessing any such ability, he could not, cannot, and will not ever have these extra-biblical effects on my life.

CHAPTER 36

Throughout elementary, junior high and high school I participated in choir and theater. I was fortunate enough to have held the lead rolls in many productions. This granted me the opportunity to acquire some singing skill. Dancing was practiced much more and was definitely not just a natural talent. However, through detailed how-to direction, patience and practice my singing and dancing held up just fine with my portrayal of characters. Acting was something I enjoyed, and I seemed to have the knack. This granted me many scholarship opportunities which did include college. I also competed with and against several people who continued aspects of theater for careers. One of my high school crushes was Rene Zellweger. If not for my commitment and monogamist heart, we would have come to know one another more personally. However, my love was genuine and true to my high school sweetheart Vanessa who I married.

So, at **The Manna House,** Ron Albright and I lead the service praise and worship. This positioned me facing the congregation. I do not recall what prompted this spontaneous event. I'm sure it was a heartfelt unction similar to those I experienced as a child. I must tell you that I am absolutely certain it was genuine and without ulterior motive. There was nothing more than a sincere motive to assist and add to the common goal of recovery.

As the music subsided there was the typical momentary silence and a beautiful lady, about Mama's age, stood up and began to pray. She was very well spoken and eloquent in her verbal petition for the group and specifically for the men of the program. There were the gracious appeals to God, Jesus and the Holy Spirit. Then it happened. Instantly the tone changed. Adamantly and seemingly with great anger, she began a new direction. *"Devil I command you and I rebuke you in the name of Jesus and declare…"* She gritted her teeth and snarled with every angry word. I do not remember her entire dissertation or her exact chosen words, but I remember how this event struck me much different than ever before.

You see we were involved in many services where the *How To's* and relevance of this type of praying were commonly given. She had followed every direction perfectly. Her stance, grip and follow through were orthodox, fundamentally sound and she never took her eye off the ball. There was just something that did not settle with me. I knew, as clearly as I know I am alive, that the devil was NO where present. I was just as positive that neither were any of his underlings. So, if he is not omnipresent, omnipotent or omniscient then he definitely could not hear her demands, commands and reprimands.

Question is, if he could, would this be a summons for his arrival? Once again, the words of Pastor Frank Lucas motivated me to find out myself.

I considered the instructions that were so commonly given in several congregations I grew up around. *"Rebuke the devil in the name of Jesus. Take authority over him and say I REBUKE YOU, SATAN, IN THE NAME OF JESUS."* These were some common words given from pulpits, and others who had heard them in churches. So, I thought it best to dissect these instructions and make sure that I understood them properly.

The first step was to get the correct definition of every word. I went to one of my favorite reference books **The Second Edition Webster's Dictionary**. Flipping to the R's, RE- REB- REBUKE….

Rebuke - V - to scold harshly, to chastise sharply…Wait! This didn't fit! If I understand simple elementary language, and I do, this doesn't fit. To say, *"I REBUKE YOU"* means NOTHING!

If you said this to me then I might question. "Really? When? Now? How?" The word rebuke is a verb describing an action. It is not the action. However, if I said, ***"You insubordinate, disrespectful excuse for a being, if you don't cease and desist your pitiful attempt to interfere with my progress I will unleash the wrath of Michael and his warriors now! Who do you think you are?"*** That is a rebuke.

Because I am a son of The King, saved by grace, made righteous by Christ Jesus, redeemed by His blood, His ambassador, and one with Him, this reprimand is in the name of Jesus. Yet, without being in the presence of the one it is intended or directed towards it is of little relevance.

CHAPTER 37

The following morning, I left for a few appointments. I believe this was one of the three events God used to solidify the declaration I made to Pastor Dan and Ron. FM 359, the Farm to Market road directly in front of the property, was under construction. The expansion was going on for months north of our address and finally made it directly in front of **The Manna House**. I was forced to turn with on-coming traffic and drive a couple of miles before turning back. My cut off was only an eye shot south, but the construction required I drive north first.

I went to cross FM 359 and my eyes were arrested by an extremely alarming sight. The man holding the Stop/Slow sign to control traffic appeared to have swallowed a python. His throat bulged, contorted and moved from mouth to tonsils and ear to ear. I drove forward with the traffic line when he flipped the slow side of the sign our direction. My eyes never left him. I imagined everyone else was staring the same way except the person driving the large Ford truck behind me. His obnoxious horn startled me.

About an hour prior to dusk I returned on the street I desired to cross to that morning. The road construction was at this intersection. There was a long precession of cars waiting to either enter or cross FM 359. The traffic attendant permitted an allotted number of cars through every few minutes. My last stop placed me third from the intersection. I immediately noticed the crossing director to be the same man with the python in his throat. I instantly rolled down my window, opened my door and stepped up in the window opening. I placed my right foot on the car seat. Standing as high as I could, I watched intently. This *thing* appearing in shape, pigment and texture to be a tongue was extended outside the man's mouth. It moved, lapped, twisted and turned as if it had a motive of its own. The man jerked his head my direction. His bulging eyes intensely observed my attention.

There is no way a tongue of this size could occupy a human mouth. It would have been cramped in a cow's jaw. Then suddenly, as if it had never been there, the abnormality disappeared. The man flipped the sign to Slow and the two cars in front of me began their advance. I was directly behind them and the man never again looked my direction. As strange as it sounds there wasn't a hint of evidence of what I had seen.

The inner unction I knew and responded to as child was there. I knew it now as I knew it then. *"YES."*

"Yes what?" I thought. Was it a demon? It had to be.

"YES" again. So deep and certain there was no questioning its origin. My mind flashed back to my stairway experience with my step- brother Billy. Only this time they didn't leave, they retreated. I assessed he was a

host and likely desired to remain that way for the time. I never saw him again, but I believe this was the incident used to reconfirm my adamant declaration.

Time and time again there have been conversations addressing my own thoughts circling this topic of the devil. I dug into resources like the Strong's Concordance, the Lexicon, Inner-Lineal Bible and the seven translations I had acquired for personal studies. I could not find biblical reference to support the *How To's* the beautiful lady and Pastor Dan demonstrated. I was beginning to believe these ideas were an extra-biblical doctrine.

CHAPTER 38

"Well Troy, anytime something happens that you don't understand – it's the enemy." I responded something like *"Come on, you can't expect me to accept that."* Her answer was *"That's what I believe and I use it to determine if it's God or the enemy."*

"So, there's NO way it could just be a lack of understanding?" I politely inquired.

This conversation was the explanation I received from a pastor's wife of 40 years. Both he and she are still highly respected pastors. They are absolutely wonderful and selfless servants of The Kingdom. I just take exception to this concept.

During the middle of an expansion project back at **The Manna House**, I was approached by a co-resident. This particular man held a part-time position as a waiter. The restaurant was located at the local mall. He began to express a few events of his day. He sat down on a stack of building material near the saw horses I was working off at that time.

He started a conversation saying *"Man, it's been a tough one Bubba."* Curious and considerate I stopped what I was doing and sat down next to him. His elbows were on his knees and his head hung down with his chin pressing against his chest.

"What's up, man?" I inquired. *"We've got a powerful enemy! I was on my break, sitting on a bench outside the restaurant in the middle of the mall. I was thinking about the Lord and suddenly, these three girls just walked right by me. They were in high heels and short skirts. The devil knows that's my weakness and he just sent them right to me. I have been doing so good Bubba."*

He was so serious I thought he was going to cry. *"And, you think 'THE DEVIL' specifically sent those young girls walking by you at that moment just to do what?"*

"To make me sin, what else! I haven't been able to think straight since." Considering his current emotions, I said *"That's the stupidest thing I've ever heard, Bro."* I stood up and began to grab, stack and position all the lumber I could get my hands on as to fashion a make-shift alter.

"Let's build this alter so you can continue your 'Devil Worship.'"

Once again, a bold declaration blurted without thought. I wasn't kind or gentle with my statement. There wasn't a tinge of compassion either. If anything, I was revolted by his pansy disposition and glorifying weakness. My own personal disappointments affected the way I reacted towards people for quite some time. Thank God I've moved past those displays of disgust. I imagine my responses offended some people along the way.

CHAPTER 39

New Year's Eve 2004, just about dusk, we were having a fabulous bringing in the year celebration. The families and friends of most every man had joined us. Of course, it was unique for many because we were celebrating sober. Things were going very well, and I believed in a strong successful future.

Our bonfire was dying early and there wasn't sufficient wood to rebuild it. Ron and I took four or five men, jumped onto a tractor pulling a 16' trailer with hay bales and set out across the 50 acres to gather wood. After gathering all we could, dusk was past us and I assumed the need to help with lighting as Ron drove. I stood behind the driver's seat of the old Ford tractor. Holding on with my left hand I lit the path over Ron's right shoulder with a rechargeable Q-Beam. Suddenly; well I only remember the trailer being lifted off me. I was sitting with my legs forward, bent at the waist and my head between my knees.

"Hun, I need you to roll over on your left side. I'm going to place this back-brace underneath you, roll you on it and then we'll secure the breast plate with its Velcro straps."

My back was broken in three places, seven ribs fractured, lungs bruised, and my body had many scrapes. I was overwhelmed with grave fear. I had been transferred to Herman Memorial Hospital in the Medical Center of Houston, Texas. The first examination at Christus Saint Catherine of Katy, Texas was scary. The doctor was kind, but he explained the injury was too severe for their facility. I don't recall much of the commute from the accident to the hospital, nor from hospital to hospital. I do recall my sister, Dee Anne, being there when I was wheeled in strapped to the stretcher. She remained with me until I was transported to the Medical Center.

In and out of the morphine sedation, I communicated the best I could with my visitors the next day. Michelle and her husband, Marty, Dee Anne and Frank, and of course, Mama and Papa T were all there. What I remember were the laughs and comments from my wonderful brother in-laws about the humorous effects of the pain killers.

Although I did my typical cutting up and attempting to make light of the peril, I am confident my sedated state was more entertaining than me.

"Are you strapping me up so we can go dancing, darling?" I asked the nurse. *"Today I just want you to sit up and take two steps to this chair. If you do okay, then I'd like you to eat your lunch sitting up."* The physical therapist was a very attractive and kind lady. She explained how the doctors' staff would decide in the next 48 hours if I would undergo surgery. As she spoke I became obstinate and rebelled against every word. *"Listen, ma'am, I'm not going to sit there in that chair until you and I go dancing."* She chuckled very kindly and gave

an audible to complete my suiting up. She placed the breast plate on top and cinched the Velcro straps firm.

"I'm going to help move your legs to the side of the bed and you sit up at the same time."

I followed her direction and was sitting on the side of the bed with my legs hanging off. At 5'6" and a 30" inseam my short legs didn't quite reach the floor. She wheeled the stand that my IV hung on so that I could use it as a support to assist my dismount. She then explained how she would hold my other arm to assist me with the two-step destination. My feet hit the floor and I put one foot in front of the other. My determination was much stronger than her mild gesture toward the chair. I was headed for the door. I was in a room about dead center of the walk area circling the nurses' station of the Critical Care Unit.

"Just right here. You only need to sit and eat your lunch."

"No, ma'am, not till after you and I dance." Putting one foot in front of the other I began to recall every detail of the faith exercise.

"NOW faith is! Right now, I am healed and right now, I am whole! Either Jesus fully accomplished His work, or He died in vain, and JESUS DID NOT DIE IN VAIN!"

I built an inner image of perfect healing. My mind zipped through every daily affirmation of my identity in Christ. Instantly, every detail, every aspect, every promise was MINE!

Simultaneously, I greeted each nurse. I announced to the eldest of the nurses that she was my next dance. I asked the pretty young lady next to her to pick a special song for her dance. Everyone smiled but there seemed to be an air of concern rather than laughter.

"You ladies get ready, 'cause I won't take no for an answer." I declared.

My escort encouraged me by saying, *"You are doing well, but I don't want you to wear yourself out. Your lungs are bruised pretty badly.*

We'll have to work on that before you walk too much."

"A good polka always gives the lungs a workout. Do you polka, or should I get one of these other ladies?" I had cautiously inched about three quarters of the way back around.

A team of doctors and interns entered the CC Unit. By this time the entrance was at our back. I continued around as the nurse attempted to nudge me toward my room.

"Look, ma'am, I'm okay." Gesturing at the doctors behind me I continued *"They are going to take me out of this CC Unit today and I'm going home in a few days from now. You're going to be begging these doctors to send me home, I promise."*

We went around the nurses' station one more time. I sat up, ate lunch and was moved to a regular room before the end of that day. At the end of the fifth day that very sweet physical therapist was standing outside my room telling the lead doctor to send me home before I got sick. It wasn't a surprise to me. I knew it before I ever heard my own words. I knew it, and as the result, the words just came out. I experienced a miracle. I believe more than one. However, my experience wasn't God's best. Nor was it the devil's attack. I made a poor decision.

My most unfortunate attribute is my bull-headed stubborn ability to continue making poor decisions. I was back at **The Manna House** in full swing. I was climbing ladders, hauling sheet metal above my head and carrying on as if the molded hardened plastic, Velcro breast plate and back piece didn't even exist. The culmination of fear and my bull- headed super hero mentality just didn't jell for a continued relationship with **The Manna House**. My residence there ended.

CHAPTER 40

There is another scenario I have used countless times. Our mind is amazing. We are astonishingly advanced in technology, science, medicine, communication, and on and on. However, we are limited in simple conceptions, especially when it comes to basic words. So, read this carefully.

Johnny is an unstable young man. He appears disturbed and uncomfortable in most every circumstance. He's become aggressive and angry about every aspect of life. Now that he is in his mid- teenage years he has chosen a direction of terror and destruction. He is known in school as a trouble maker. He's already known by the local police and has been questioned in several break-ins, burglaries and other criminal activity. His name is the constant chatter of his community.

"Johnny is evil. He only wants to hurt people, steal and destroy things. He was the one who made my tires flat and put the crack in my windshield. I know it was Johnny who shot my dog."

"Our whole community is going down because of Johnny. He is very cunning and sneaky. He's putting all these bad ideas into our children's minds."

"We have to be careful of Johnny and know his ways because he's constantly attacking us all. Everywhere we go, everything we see, and in everything we hear, Johnny is in it. He is taking our whole world to hell in a hand basket."

This community commonly gathered to discuss the horrific state of the town. By their discussion's default they may as well change the hometown name to **"Hopelessly Doomed."** The only thing unified was their general consensus of *"**Johnny Worship**."* Their conversations praised him for his accomplishments, glorified his terror, magnified his malice, exalted his madness and honored his horror.

Near the front, a tall, well built, good-looking dark-haired man in his late thirties stood to his feet. He raised both his hands just above his shoulders. Clinched in his right hand was a well-read and tattered book. His thunderous baritone voice brought the room to a silence. He had everyone's attention. *"Excuse me, I'm new in town but my family goes all the way back to our founding fathers. They left me an inheritance which includes our stake right in 'Hometown.' I have never lived here myself, but I have your town history right here."* There was a rumble of low voices attempting to calculate what the stranger was going to say. *"According to what is written, Johnny was defeated, run out of town, his works rendered to naught, stripped of all power and authority and 'Hometown' was given back to us over 2,000 years ago!"*

This scenario may seem humorous, but it depicts exactly what I witnessed in many church settings and among Christian friends. And the good-looking dark-haired man sited the absolute of our inheritance.

CHAPTER 41

You may not be familiar with these small Christian tracks, but they were common literature among the circles we frequented. They almost appear to be comic books. Illustrational art with word filled bubbles above the characters are on the slender pages. These tracks are about 3" tall and 5" long. Their rectangular pages are held together with staples. They are packed with end times dooms day stories and many scared straight tactics. We learned about all kinds of devil worship and satanic things. It is highly probable I would have never known symbols, signs or markings that referenced evil if not for these recommended readings. Conversations, sermons and the not so uncommon explanations of these blood bath sacrificial demonic events sculpted imaginations. If anyone would know about devil worship, it was us.

The staggering truth about this superior education was how it became a fundamental aspect. *Devil Worship*, accrediting problems and undesired emotions to the devil, in the church seemed to take on the same importance as proper *Christianeze*.

"Praise the Lord, the devil's really been attacking me lately." "The devil has been coming against me really strong, but God is faithful." These and many, many others were just common expressions heard in the church arenas we traveled. I was becoming convinced the average Christian knew more about the devil and his escapades than who they are in Christ. My recollection of the most common remark concerning unfavorable events was *"Well, that's just the devil!"*

This blanket comment seemed to relieve or negate all responsibility, thus giving the recipient a since of ease with this granted outlet of blame and dismissal of fault. I suppose that was the purpose of such lunacy and disinformation. Most unexplainable about this mainstream dogma was its hands down acceptance. This explanation directly opposing the primary basics of maturity and is a cop out rebelling against the oracle of responsibility. The exact essence of what we strive to train our children to be is snuffed and scoffed with this dysfunctional devil doctrine. Success, achievement, accomplishment, character and honor are only obtained by taking responsibility for our decisions and actions. Taking responsibility is the foundation of growth, yet the institution God set to build and establish us is crippled with extra-biblical ideals of the devil.

CHAPTER 42

About a year after I left **The Manna House** my life began to spin out of control again and Mama had an unacceptable idea.

"Mama you know how much I love you, but I am finished with ministries."

"Just please call them for me, son."

I cannot tell you if Mama knew the power behind this statement. There isn't a thing I wouldn't give my greatest effort towards if requested by Mama. Unfortunately, most my efforts were inhibited by the grip of addiction. What I wanted seemed to be the things I couldn't produce nor the power to accomplish them.

She went on to explain that she heard about the place from **Kenneth Copeland Ministries**. Of course, if her 'for me' request didn't finalize her sale then its origin would seal the deal.

"Why don't you see if they might have a position on staff?"

I took the information and followed her inside. As you may have already envisioned, she handed me the phone. The instant I completed my phone call Mama popped back into the room and inquired what was said. I explained how they had no openings on staff and how they didn't really hire anyone because most staff were graduates.

"Son, I know you don't want to hear this, but…."

I cringed at the thought of what was coming next. We both knew that it would only take a couple of phone calls and I would be right back in the automotive transmission repair industry.

"…I believe the Lord has told me this is where you are supposed to go."

"They don't have any positions, Mama."

"Why don't you call them back and see what it takes to get in." Mama may have been asking in her gentle kindness, but she wasn't going to settle for anything other than a *"Yes Ma'am."* While suggesting I call back, the cordless hand set went from her to me. I only had to push a single button to redial the number. Like Deja vu Mama reappeared. This time she didn't have to say a word. The question was unspoken but loud and clear.

"I was told to call back tomorrow to set an appointment. They said I needed to call at exactly 1:00 p.m." My mind raced in an attempt to find an explanation of how and why it would be unreasonable, difficult or impossible for this to work. I knew that no matter the excuse Mama had a solution. I would not miss that 1:00 p.m. marker. I informed the answering voice who I was and why I was calling. I knew it wouldn't take but a moment because I was only setting an appointment. Several minutes later a man came on the phone and began to take my personal information. He then explained how someone would be calling me for an interview and if I wasn't available I would be put to the end of the list. He went on to share that even if I was accepted there

was still a two-year waiting list. I do not recall all we spoke about, but these words will forever be seared in my consciousness.

"I don't know what it is, but I really feel the Lord telling me to get you here right now. This has never happened to me in a pre-interview."

Mentally I was now racing even faster for an escape. What could I say? What was I going tell Mama? It was obvious that someone was coordinating her efforts. I was then told I needed blood work and the test results had to be sent to him before my acceptance was final. *"Okay, where do I have the tests done and how long does it take to get the results?"*

He gave me the information on how to find a place and said it's typically a two- to three-week process. My final instructions were a weekly contact until I arrived. I disconnected the call and once again Mama was instantly there. I had the information written down and explained how I would begin my search for a lab the next day. I ended with something like *"We'll see how it goes."* I don't think ten minutes had passed and Mama came back into the kitchen to let me know we would be leaving in five minutes. *"I found a place in Katy to do the test. They will have your results today and have them faxed before they close."*

I walked out the back door and found a garbage can to take out my frustration. I kicked the container and proceeded to shout at God once again. *"Why won't you just leave me alone?"*

Mama came out the back door, purse on her shoulder and keys in hand. She knew I wasn't happy, but she assured me it was a good plan that God had for me.

My results were received, reviewed and accepted. The same man explained how he had never seen anyone accepted so fast. I cannot say that I was as pleased as he and my mother, but I was packed and loaded up for our journey through Texas, across Louisiana and Mississippi, to a small town of about 300 people called Autaugaville, Alabama.

I would arrive at **Canaan Land Ministry**.

CHAPTER 43

My first impression of **Canaan Land Ministries** was my parking lot greeting from Jon Roll and Kyle Taylor. Kyle said, *"We are glad you are here and happy to see you."* I can only imagine the expression on my face. Mama has laughed about it for years. His words seemed so canned and typical. I learned quickly that both Jon and Kyle were sincere and meant every kind word they greeted me with. Twelve years later and I am still friends with both of them.

Canaan Land Ministries is a bible training center for men with life controlling addictions. We spent the first four hours of each weekday in bible classes. The culture was great and the facility exceptional.

Every student is assigned a position of daily operation. The starting position for every new student is dish washer. I guess this was considered the bottom of the totem pole.

It was only a few weeks and I was in charge of the kitchen's full operation. The head cook was caught smoking and his residence terminated. This gave me opportunity to move into my comfort zone. I quickly began to cook full meals for all staff lunches. Baked chicken, fresh veggies, hand smashed potatoes with homemade gravy and a side salad was for starters. This rivaled the typical cold sandwich, peanut butter and jelly or a dumped can of cold green beans. Offering a daily fresh hot lunch afforded the opportunity to get to know everyone in the front office fast and personal.

Our monthly food bank and Sam's Club grocery shopping trip was scheduled about the same time I took the lead kitchen position. This responsibility included riding with **Phil Bevilacqua** to pick out the food and supplies for the upcoming month. I should let you know that part of the requirement for students was to address all staff by Mrs. or Mr., Brother, Sister, or Pastor. Grandpa had instilled a strict adherence to addressing everyone with a courteous yes sir, no sir, yes ma'am, no ma'am, Mr., Mrs., and please and thank you. This is habit and is just second nature for all in our family. I had no problem with the common Mr. and Mrs. prefix when addressing anyone. Even Brother and Sister are not unusual given our church experience; however, at this time I almost viewed Pastor as a four-letter word. First introduction to Pastor Phil and I knew we were friends. I just could not call him Pastor. I chose to call him Pops. He's a few years younger than me so he didn't know or understand why I chose this term of endearment until more than a half decade later.

We may have not even left the property and Pops said something like, *"Someone in the camp is spreading a teaching that the devil cannot put thoughts in your head."*

I immediately knew exactly what he was referring to and I knew exactly who was spreading this philosophy. Although I was also certain the person had only spoke to a couple of others, I knew there was only one person who had such an opinion. *"Well we might as well talk about that Pops because I'm the one who believes that the devil can't put thoughts in my head. I can tell you that there is not one verse in the Bible that supports the idea. It's an extra-biblical belief. If you can show me one verse that says it's possible I'll believe it. In fact, I'm even willing to make a challenge. You find one verse that says he can, and I'll find five that says it's impossible. If you find one, I'll never mention it again."* My challenge may not have been said exactly this way and I'm sure the conversation was longer, but this is what was conveyed.

I remember our conversations to be personal and enlightening. From this day forward, he is my friend. We talked about Righteousness, Redemption, Forgiveness, that Jesus is the once for all sacrifice and absolutely nothing is left for us to accomplish. He did it all. I think I talked mostly, and Pops dug out my thoughts with curious inquisition.

CHAPTER 44

Less than a week later while taking lunch orders in the front office a young lady came out of her office to confront me. She vehemently exclaimed that the devil can put thoughts in her head and insisted I explain the voices she heard. I was taken back but kindly began to answer when suddenly I heard,

"It's extra-biblical; there is no place in the bible that says the devil can put thoughts in your head." It was **Phil Bevilacqua**. We were nowhere near the agreed deadline of the challenge, but there he was saying exactly what I had shared on our first trip to the food bank.

We had many other wonderful occasions where we wrangled the word. It wasn't long and the two of us were being called on the carpet for our Righteousness Consciousness beliefs and proclamations.

Things moved fast and the opportunity to use my business building and marketing skills proved to be beneficial for **Canaan Land Ministries** and myself. There was big talk of an upcoming event that would be the fruition of a fifteen-year vision. **Eight Days of Glory** at **Canaan Land** featured its first year September of 2006. **Brother Mac** and **Ms. Sandra Gober** had loved many men through twenty-eight years of ministry and had dreamed of this event for most of those years.

"Eight, that's God's number for New Beginnings," Brother Mac told us over and over again. It had to be a great success and I believed I had much to offer in ensuring a grand event.

There were expansion building projects, remodeling, clean up, painting and much more. The biggest necessity for marketing would be the media blast campaign. I could see the detail of need and began to make a list of each category.

I shared my observations with Ms. Sandra and a listed plan I believed would address each category. In short term I was appointed as the Ministries Administrator. As the result of our administrative accomplishments, **Brother Mac** honored me and several others in a most remarkable way. Closing night of **Eight Days of Glory** we were ordained by **Brother Kenneth Copeland**!

CHAPTER 45

You are God's will, His purpose and His pleasure. Everything He has done, all that He is and all He has are just for you. You need not toil or strive to be in God's will. You are the will of God! He has nothing He wants you to do for Him; however, He has an amazing destiny He desires to live WITH you!!

I became a full-fledged drug addict. I hurt many people and have done many wrong things. If there is anyone who has experienced the truth of God's Grace, it is me. God has never been angry, upset or disappointed. He has never left me, turned His back on me or left me to my own demise. He never *allowed* me to go through things to teach me nor caused negative things to direct me. It is not in His nature.

Here is a fact. God never had to forgive me for anything I have done. He forgave me once and forgave me for all in Jesus that day at Calvary. I am His son even in the middle of all my wrongs. There is no bad thing I could ever do that could out do the work of the Cross. This is true for you too.

I want to invite you to join us in this journey of **Amazing Real Hope**. We will spend the rest of this life-giving Hope to the Hopeless and pulling men from addiction to significance. We are launching **Amazing Real Hope** to fulfill a vision God gave to me in 2006 while at **Canaan Land Ministries**. Thank you, **Brother Mac** and **Ms. Sandra**. We owe you a life of gratitude. I owe that same gratitude to my family, everyone I wrote of and many more. I desire to give others what all of you have given me.

I hope you have enjoyed this journey in the memoirs of my life and I look forward to sharing many more for the rest of our lives journey. I invite you to help change the world in a life time by partnering with us at **Amazing Real Hope**. Our commitment to you is to never let go, never ostracize, condemn or criticize anyone for any reason. Jesus said, *"It is the will of the Father that I not lose one."* This is the will of God for us too, and our commitment to every one of our partners.

If you don't have the **Amazing Real Hope** of Jesus please pray the prayer on the next page and you too will know His Love.

PRAYER TO SALVATION

God, I believe Jesus. I believe He died and rose again for me. I believe in You and want to know how real You are. Make Your life known to me, so I will have Amazing Real Hope in Jesus. Show me Your Love and give me Your eternal life. In the name of Jesus, I receive all of You. Thank You for loving me too.

Amen

Remember you are living in The Lord Jesus Christ and He is living in you. I encourage you to join a local church, get involved in church community and follow us for continuing understanding of who you are in Christ Jesus.

ABOUT THE FOUNDATION

Amazing Real Hope supports world and local missions who instill hope to the hurting and hopeless. We feature a revolutionary faith-based recovery community for addicts and alcoholics. We offer Theophostic and Therapon counseling, accredited bible classes and a premiere entrepreneurship program while participating in equine therapy, business operation, economics, etiquette and much more.

Troy Ingenhuett

www.amazingrealhope.com

troyingehuett@amazingrealhope.com

936-435-4905

Made in the USA
Columbia, SC
19 February 2019